Copyright©MCMLXXXV by World International Publishing Limited.
All rights reserved throughout the world.
1985 edition published by Derrydale Books
Distributed by Crown Publishers, Inc.
hgfedeba
Library of Congress Cataloguing-in-Publication Data
Main entry under title:
Questions and Answers: 2 volumes in 1.
Previously published separately under title: 201 Children's Questions
and Answers and Children's Questions and Answers.
Summary: Hundreds of questions and answers on a wide range of topics.
1. Children's Questions and Answers. [1. Questions and Answers]
I. 201 Children's Questions and Answers. 1985. II. Children's
Questions and Answers. 1985.
AG195.   Q45 1985   631'.02   85-15883
ISBN 0-517-47999-0
Printed in Hungary.

315 CHILDREN'S
QUESTIONS
and
ANSWERS

Written by Lesley Scott and Brenda Apsley.
Illustrated by Jane Cunningham.

DERRYDALE BOOKS
New York

Why do dogs bury bones?

Dogs have been at people's side for longer than any other animal. But a lot of their actions can only be explained by their past before they were tamed by humans. For example, you may have noticed that a dog turns round three times on the spot before settling down to sleep – this may be because its ancestors had to flatten down a nest in the leaves of the forests or jungles where they lived, before they could sleep. And when a dog stands and bays, it may be doing what its ancestors did when they roamed in packs and had to keep in touch with one another. The same may be true of the bone burying routine. Before people fed dogs regularly, they had to hunt for food themselves, and burying it was the best way of keeping what they found, where their sense of smell could easily find it again.

Are elephants afraid of mice?

Although you may have seen many cartoons and films which show elephants being terrified by tiny mice, in reality elephants pay as little attention to mice, which often scuttle around their feet, as you would pay a sparrow in your garden or in the street. Many people believe that the elephant would be afraid of the mouse because it is small enough to crawl up inside the elephant's trunk and suffocate it. This has almost definitely never happened. If it did, the elephant could easily draw a breath and blow the mouse out again.

Why does the camel have a hump?

The camel's best known nickname is 'the ship of the desert', and it is very well suited to the camel. The camel is ideally suited to the life it leads in the desert, and its best adaptation is its hump.

Although many people know that the camel can go for days, even weeks at a time, without food or water, not many know how the camel manages it. Before a long journey, the camel's owner makes sure that the creature is very well-fed and has drunk a lot of water. The hump at that moment is upright and stiff. When the journey is over, the camel's hump is loose and flabby. What has happened? The food that the camel ate before it set out was turned into reserves of fat, and stored in the hump, while the water was kept in tiny, flask-shaped sacs in the camel's stomach. During the journey, the camel used these stores to keep itself going, and when the trip was over, it had to spend a long time getting its strength back.

Who was Cleopatra?

Cleopatra was the queen of Egypt at the time of Julius Caesar, and was supposed to have been one of the most beautiful women in the world. When very young, she was deposed from her throne, and Caesar, who fell in love with her, helped her regain it. She bore him a son, Caesarion, and went to Rome with him, returning to Egypt when he died. Cleopatra then fell in love with Mark Antony, a very powerful Roman, who was a close friend of Caesar's and one of the rivals for the title of Emperor. Mark Antony left his wife, who was the sister of the other contender, later the Emperor Augustus, and went to Egypt. Augustus was furious, and waged war on his rivals. They were defeated, and committed suicide rather than be captured, Cleopatra supposedly holding an asp to her arm and dying of its bite.

What was the Piltdown Man?

At the beginning of this century, a workman in a gravel pit in Sussex, England, found what looked like a coconut. On closer inspection, he found it to be a skull, and he handed it over to a local fossil collector. This man, Charles Dawson, became wildly excited about it. He believed that he had in his hands the skull of the Missing Link.

Since Darwin had propounded his ideas of Man's evolution from apes, a Missing Link had been searched for, a bridge between apes and humans that would prove the theory once and for all. Now it was believed that it was found. But the Piltdown Man, as it was called, was a fake. Its jawbone was that of a chimpanzee, its skull that of a prehistoric man, and the two had cleverly been put together. But who could have pulled off such a trick? No one has ever found out!

What is an eclipse of the sun?

A total eclipse of the sun happens when the moon and the earth are in direct alignment with the sun, so that light is blocked off by the moon completely. In a small area it goes totally dark, as if it is night, while in a much larger area, a dusk falls. This has strange effects on the life of the planet. During a total eclipse, blood seems to take a much longer time to clot, primitive peoples panic, and animals become extremely agitated.

Why do men wear beards?

For centuries a man's beard was regarded as a sign of manhood, wisdom and strength, but at various times in history shaving has become fashionable. After a tour of Europe at the end of the 17th century Peter the Great of Russia decided that his people should follow the example of the Europeans and be clean shaven, so he introduced a tax on beards. Many Russians, however, were proud of their beards and refused to shave. Peter the Great fined them heavily, and had the beards forcibly shaved off!

How many people have ever lived?

A huge number! Imagine all the people who are alive today, if you can. Then imagine this — that for every living person, there are thirty dead ones!

Who was the first man to reach the North Pole?

Robert Edwin Peary, an American, became the first man to reach the North Pole on 6th April 1909. He was accompanied by a dog-driver and three Eskimos, and travelled by sledge.

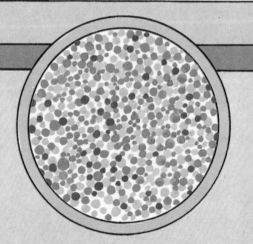

What is color blindness?

Color blindness is a condition of the eyes where certain colors become indistinguishable from each other, and are sometimes seen as shades of gray. The most common sort of color blindness is that which confuses red and green, and this is far more common in men than in women.

What is Valhalla?

Valhalla is an old Norse word meaning *the hall of the slain*. This was the place where the spirits of dead Norse heroes went. They were served with wonderful food and drink, and the hall itself was built of gold, while armour and shields hung on the walls and reflected the light so brightly that candles were not needed.

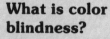

Why are ravens kept at the Tower of London?

There is a legend which says that if the ravens should ever leave the Tower of London, the White Tower will collapse and disaster will come to England. There are six ravens at the Tower, and they are cared for by one of the Yeomen of the Guard.

How many bees are there in a beehive?

A beehive is a very crowded, busy place. There may be as many as 60,000 bees in one hive!

Is there such a thing as a giant squid?

Yes, there is, although you won't find one wrapping itself around the nearest sailing ship! The largest giant squid ever found was one measuring 55 feet (16.7 m) in total length – its tentacles alone were 35 feet (10.6 m) long!

Is the owl really wise?

In fact, it isn't! For its size, the owl has a small brain, and is less intelligent than geese, crows and ravens.

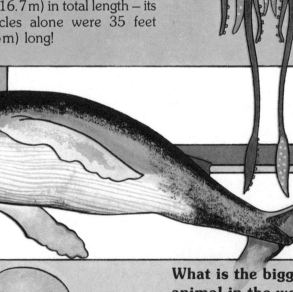

What is the fastest land animal?

The cheetah is the animal kingdom's fastest runner. It can run at speeds of 70 mph, and so is a successful hunter. Natives of Asia and Africa have sometimes caught and trained cheetahs to hunt for them.

How many muscles are there in the human body?

639 – the same for males and females.

What is the biggest animal in the world?

The largest and heaviest animal in the world is the Blue Whale, which is also believed to be the largest animal that has *ever* lived. The biggest example ever found was over 110 feet (33.5 m) long, and weighed over 170 tons (172 tonnes).

Do scarecrows really scare birds away?

Farmers traditionally make a 'man' from poles and straw and dress him in old clothes in the hope that the scarecrow will scare birds from the fields. When the practice began the birds were scared away, but they soon became used to the figures. What has been found to work is a figure that *moves,* and modern mechanical scarecrows are now available. Other successful bird-scarers are tapes of bird distress cries played at regular intervals, and radio-controlled hawk-shaped flying models.

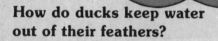

Is the tomato a fruit or a vegetable?

It is classified as a fruit because it has seeds inside its juicy pulp, like berry fruits. Cucumbers are also classified as fruits.

What is the fastest dog?

The greyhound is the fastest dog. It can reach speeds of 40mph.

How do ducks keep water out of their feathers?

Birds that live constantly in water, like ducks or swans, have a small gland on their backs called an oil gland. This produces a kind of oil which is wiped all over the duck's feathers when it preens. It is very effective, as it keeps the water out of the feathers and also provides the duck with valuable vitamin D.

Why don't spiders get caught in their own webs?

Spiders use two different kinds of thread to spin their webs. Sticky threads capture their prey and other, silky threads enable the spider to move around the web.

What is a basenji?

A basenji is a dog with a difference – it cannot bark. The breed dates back to about 3,000 BC, when they were used very effectively as hunting dogs.

What is the tallest animal in the world?

The giraffe, which is up to 18 ft (5.5 m) tall.

Do all snakes lay eggs?

No, not all of them. A large number of snakes do lay eggs – the python, for example – and some lay up to 100 at a time. But there are others who give birth to live young – these include rattlesnakes, water snakes and copperheads.

What is the largest office block in the world?

The Pentagon, the headquarters of the United States government's Department of Defense, in Washington DC. The Pentagon, as its name implies, is five-sided, and has five storeys. If you were to walk along every one of its passages, you would cover $17\frac{1}{2}$ miles (28 kilometres), and over 29,000 people work within its walls.

What is Surtsey?

In 1963 there was a volcanic eruption in the sea just off the southern coast of Iceland. The lava it threw up cooled and hardened to form the new island of Surtsey. Nobody lives there, but the plants and insects that have started to live there make it a fascinating place for scientists to study.

Who invented the toothbrush?

A man called William Addis. Whilst serving a term in London's Newgate Prison Addis was cleaning his teeth with a rag (the method then used) when he had an idea. He got a small meat bone, put some tiny holes in it, then put small bunches of broom bristles through the holes. He found that this toothbrush worked very well, and after his release from prison set up a successful toothbrush manufacturing business.

How long was the first flight?

In 1903 Orville and Wilbur Wright were testing their aircraft in North Carolina, USA. Orville was the pilot, while his brother watched the craft, *Flyer,* career through space for twelve seconds before touching down again. This was the first powered flight in history, and the distance *Flyer* travelled is shorter than the wingspan of a modern jumbo jet!

Who invented esperanto?

Esperanto is a special language, invented so that people of all nationalities can talk together and correspond. It is taught in some schools, but has not had the success that its inventor, a Polish doctor called Ludovic Zamenhof, hoped for when he developed it in 1887.

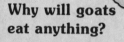

Which two countries are connected by the Mont Blanc Tunnel?

France and Italy. The great, snow-capped mountain of Mont Blanc was something of a barrier between the two countries until work started on a tunnel that was excavated through seven miles (11 kilometres) of solid rock. It was finally opened in 1965.

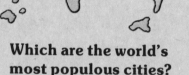

Why will goats eat anything?

We're really not too sure, but it seems that the reason is that they feel unloved! Goats have never had the care and attention bestowed on other domestic animals, and will attempt to eat almost anything in the hope that it's good, since they are not usually fed well.

Which are the world's most populous cities?

New York (USA), Tokyo (Japan) and Shanghai (China) are the world's most heavily-populated cities. More than 11,000,000 people live in each city. London is home to some 7,000,000 people.

Who was the first Marathon runner?

This was a Greek called Pheidippides, in 490 BC, who ran over 26 miles (42 kilometers) in 4 hours to take the news to Athens that the Greek army had beaten the Persians at the battle of Marathon.

Who built the Taj Mahal?

Considered one of the finest pieces of architecture in the world, the Taj Mahal was built as a tomb by Mogul Emperor Shah Jehan in memory of his wife. Twenty thousand workmen toiled day and night for 22 years before the building was completed in 1654.

What is a Duckbilled Platypus?

The platypus is a very strange-looking animal, having the fur of a mammal and a duck-like beak. Platypuses are mammals, but they belong to a very small group called *monotremes,* which lay eggs instead of giving birth to live young. When the eggs hatch and the young appear they are weaned, like other young mammals, on the mother's milk.

Do jellyfish have a brain?

The jellyfish — which is actually an animal — does not have a brain. Muscles on the underside open and close, propelling it through the water, and tentacles reach out for food. A paralysing stab stuns tiny sea creatures and the tentacles draw the food into the mouth. The jellyfish doesn't have a heart, either, but still it is able to exist successfully.

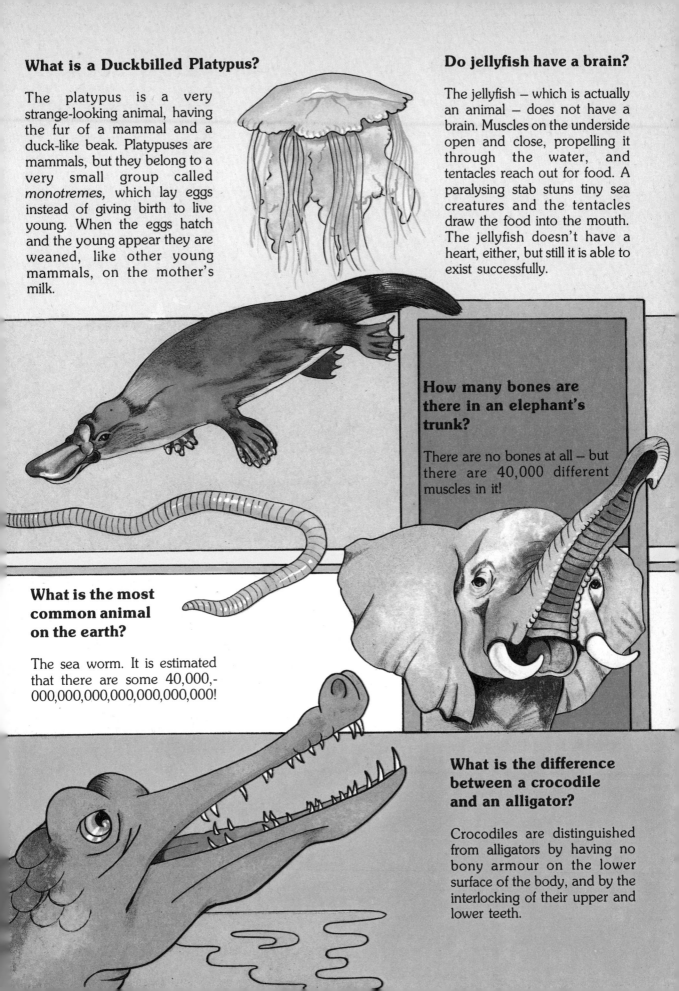

How many bones are there in an elephant's trunk?

There are no bones at all — but there are 40,000 different muscles in it!

What is the most common animal on the earth?

The sea worm. It is estimated that there are some 40,000,-000,000,000,000,000,000,000!

What is the difference between a crocodile and an alligator?

Crocodiles are distinguished from alligators by having no bony armour on the lower surface of the body, and by the interlocking of their upper and lower teeth.

Who was Nostradamus?

Nostradamus was a Frenchman who had an extraordinary talent for predicting the future. Although he lived in the sixteenth century, he could see centuries ahead, accurately predicting the lives of Napoleon, Louis Pasteur and Hitler, and seeing the damage caused to Nagasaki and Hiroshima by the atomic bombs dropped on them during the Second World War.

Who is the most popular author of all time?

Although more copies of the Bible have been printed than any other book, the world's best-selling book by a single author is *Quotations from the Works of Chairman Mao Tse-Tung,* the former Chinese leader who died in 1976. More than 800 million copies of this book have been printed!

What is the mystery of the *Mary Celeste?*

The *Mary Celeste* was a sailing ship which left New York for Genoa in 1872, and was found near Gibraltar drifting aimlessly. Everything on board was normal, the cargo intact, the sails set. Only the crew were missing, together with the captain and the captain's family. In fact, nobody was aboard the ship – and nobody has ever found out what happened to them, because they were never seen again.

What is the most valuable painting in the world?

This is the *Mona Lisa,* by Leonardo da Vinci, which was painted in about 1503-7 and shows Madonna Lisa Gherardini. Her husband disliked the painting and refused to buy it. Later, King Francis I of France bought it for the equivalent of $440,000. Now, it is worth about $50 million!

When was the tuxedo first worn?

The tuxedo is a short, tailless jacket, often with satin lapels, and is sometimes called a smoking or dinner jacket. It was first worn by a man rejoicing in the splendid name of Griswold Lorillard, at the autumn ball of the Tuxedo Park Club in New York on 10 October 1886. The fashion caught on, and the tuxedo is still very popular today.

When was khaki first used?

In the 1840s Lieutenant Harry Lumsden was forming a force in northern India, and was given permission to dress his men as he saw fit. He had cloth specially dyed to match the dusty colour of the ground, so that the men would be as inconspicuous as possible, and this colour, and the cloth too, was called khaki, after the Urdu word meaning dusty.

Who invented the flower buttonhole?

When Queen Victoria attended a gathering with her future husband, Prince Albert, she was presented with flowers, and gave one to Albert. He had nowhere to put it, so he cut a small slit in his lapel and put the flower in it. After that men started to wear flowers in specially-sewn lapel buttonholes.

Who was Angelo Faticoni?

Born in America in 1859, Angelo was a human physical phenomenon – he could not sink! Though he was examined by many doctors, nobody knew why he was so at home in water. He could sleep floating in water, even with heavy weights strapped to his ankles, and he once swam across the Hudson River strapped to a chair loaded with lead! No wonder they called him the 'human cork'.

Why do cats' eyes shine in the dark?

Like humans, cats' eyes respond to light. In the dark, a cat's pupils will open wide to let in as much light as possible. This light is reflected by a layer of cells called the *tapetum*, which is coloured pink, gold, blue or green. When the outside light alters, the tapetum acts as a mirror and reflects a different colour. This process enables cats to see about seven times better than humans can in the dark.

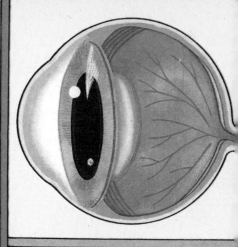

What is a liger?

A liger, like a tigon, is the very rare offspring of a crossing between a lion and a tiger. If the father is a lion and the mother a tigress, the cub will be called a liger; if the father is a tiger and the mother a lioness, then the cub will be called a tigon. These are very rare in the animal kingdom – and there are in fact only about half a dozen ligers or tigons in the world.

Which animal spits when it is angry?

The llama of South America is one animal which has this characteristic – and so does its relative, the camel. Both spit foul-smelling saliva through their teeth to defend themselves, and to show anger or annoyance. They have both been known to spit on teasing visitors at the zoo – so be warned!

Why do some people have curly hair and others straight hair?

Each hair on your body has two parts – the root under the skin, and the shaft, the part you can see. If you looked at a shaft of your hair under the microscope, it would either be round or flat. If round, you would have straight hair, and if flat, your hair would be either wavy or curly. The flatter the shaft, the curlier the hair!

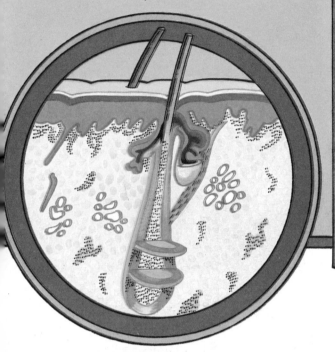

Why did sailors wear earrings?

Sailors, pirates and sea-going men used to wear earrings in the old days for two reasons. The first was a very old superstition that earrings protected them from evil spirits, and the second was a belief that their eyesight would improve and become stronger. Well, when was the last time you saw a pirate wearing glasses?

What was the shortest letter ever written?

It was written by Victor Hugo, the famous French author. He wanted to know how his book entitled *Les Miserables* was selling, so he wrote to his publisher: ?

What was the shortest reply ever written?

That came from Hugo's publisher, whose equally brief letter read: !

Who was the world's first stamp collector?

That honor belongs to a lady who placed an advertisement in *The Times* newspaper in 1841. She wanted to wallpaper her bedroom wall in used postage stamps, and appealed for them to be sent to her. Thus she became the world's first collector, though later collectors (philatelists) stuck their stamps in albums, rather than on walls! The first postage stamps in the world had been issued in Great Britain the previous year, 1840. They were called 'penny blacks' for their value and color.

How big is the Milky Way?

The galaxy we call the Milky Way is a lot bigger than we think. Our solar system, including the sun, moon and all the planets, is tiny in comparison; in the rest of the Milky Way there are over 200,000,000,000 stars. To get a better idea of its size, think of the speed at which light travels. It takes eight minutes for light from the sun to reach the earth. But it takes 100,000 YEARS for light to travel from one end of the Milky Way to the other!

Do mice really like cheese?

In stories and cartoons mice are always attracted to cheese above all things, and traps are traditionally baited with cheese. But mice are rodents, and really prefer a diet of vegetables and grains. However, a hungry mouse will eat almost anything – and that includes cheese.

Why do we blow out candles on birthday cakes?

This widespread custom of blowing out candles on someone's birthday is a very ancient one. Really it is a test of strength – is the growing child strong enough to blow out a greater number of candles every year? Though previously a test, it is now just an enjoyable custom.

What are gargoyles for?

Gargoyles are those grotesque stone heads, part-human, part-animal, that we see on the roof edges of old cathedrals and churches. They are not there to frighten people, however – in fact their useful purpose was combined with a practical joke.

Gargoyles are waterspouts, which catch the rain as it flows off the roof. The water collects in the spout of the gargoyle's mouth and is spat out into the street below, rather than dripping down the walls and causing erosion. The practical joke is apparent in the ugly faces. It is thought that the stoneworkers represented their friends' faces in these grotesque heads – I wonder if they were friends afterwards!

Why do onions make you cry?

A person peeling and chopping onions is often reduced to tears, not because they're upset, but due to the very strong smell of onions. Onions contain a very strong oil, and when they are cut the oil escapes as tiny particles of moisture, called vapour. When this vapour reaches your nose it irritates the very sensitive membranes in your nostrils. They in turn irritate the tear ducts in your eyes, and tears are produced. So it's the smell of onions that makes you cry. There are many ideas put forward to stop onions making you cry – cutting them under running water, rubbing the knife with lemon etc – but the most foolproof is to wear a scuba diving mask in the kitchen!

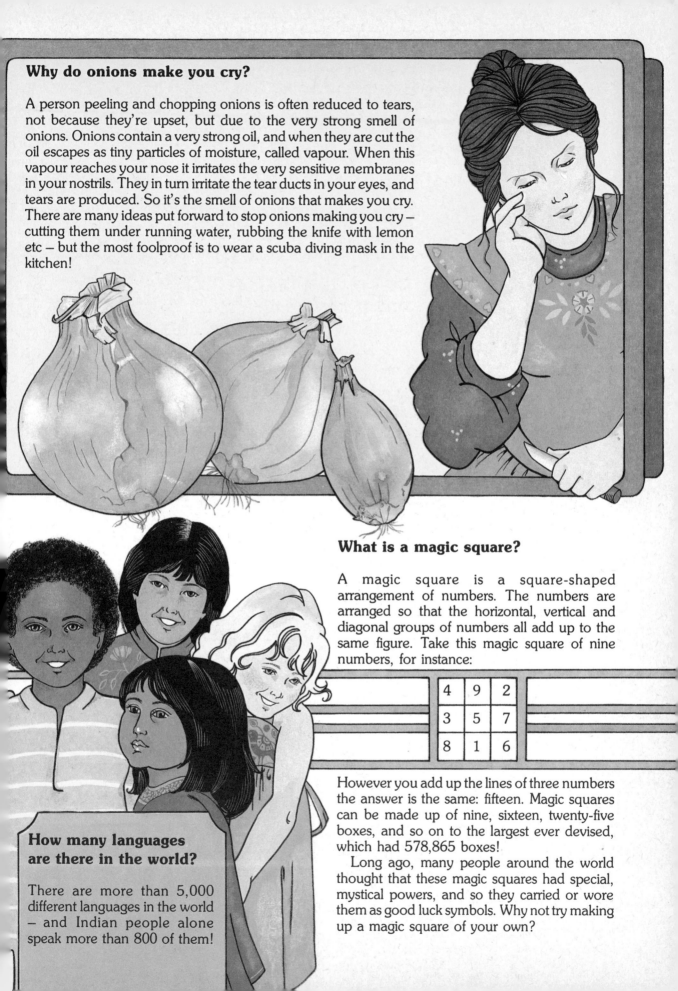

What is a magic square?

A magic square is a square-shaped arrangement of numbers. The numbers are arranged so that the horizontal, vertical and diagonal groups of numbers all add up to the same figure. Take this magic square of nine numbers, for instance:

4	9	2
3	5	7
8	1	6

However you add up the lines of three numbers the answer is the same: fifteen. Magic squares can be made up of nine, sixteen, twenty-five boxes, and so on to the largest ever devised, which had 578,865 boxes!

Long ago, many people around the world thought that these magic squares had special, mystical powers, and so they carried or wore them as good luck symbols. Why not try making up a magic square of your own?

How many languages are there in the world?

There are more than 5,000 different languages in the world – and Indian people alone speak more than 800 of them!

Why did the woolly mammoth die out?

Woolly mammoths, those strange hairy elephants, became extinct about 17,000 years ago, when the earth was extremely cold. Looking at one, you might think that it was extremely well protected against the cold, and you would be right. Extreme cold was not the problem at all.

At about this time, the glaciers which covered much of the Northern Hemisphere receded, leaving vast tracts of land covered with snow. And it was this snow that killed the mammoths. There are many reasons for this – lack of food, the mammoth's inability to walk on the deep snow, the waterlogging of the mammoth's hairy coat and so on – which all combined to cause its extinction, where other animals could adapt themselves to these treacherous conditions.

What is the fastest grower in the plant kingdom?

Bamboo. Some species grow as much as 3′ (1m) in a single day, and they can reach heights of 120′ (36m). Although bamboo looks like a tree, it is classified as a grass.

Which is the most successful pop group?

Not surprisingly, the Beatles. John Lennon, Paul McCartney, George Harrison and Ringo Starr had so many hits that in 1980 it was thought that they had sold over 100 million singles and over 100 million albums. They also won 42 gold discs.

Are there such things as vampires?

Of course not, except in books and films! Or are there? Recently American doctors in Florida have noticed that when the moon is in its second quarter, some patients bleed up to twice as much during operations . . .

Do all camels come from Africa?

Camels with one hump – Arabian camels or dromedaries – come from North Africa, but Bactrian or two-humped camels come from Asia.

Who made the Grand Canyon?

Nobody made it! The Grand Canyon was carved out by the waters of the Colorado River as it rushed along over thousands of years. And the Colorado is still cutting away at the rock of the canyon, showing us even more of the remarkable rock layers that tell the story of the earth's formation.

When did people first wear glasses?

Many people wear glasses or contact lenses these days to correct faulty vision – but glasses are nothing new; Chinese people wore lenses to improve vision as far back as 500 BC.

For what is Joseph Lister famous?

Lister was a surgeon who produced an antiseptic solution to be used during operations. Up to that time (1865) operations were mostly successful, but patients often died from infections caused by germs entering the wound. Lister's antiseptic helped prevent these infections.

How much are you worth?

In purely mineral terms, the commercial value of the water and chemicals that make up your body would be only a few pence, although to your family and friends you're worth your weight in gold!

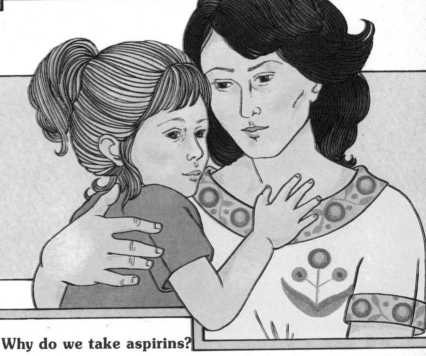

Why do we take aspirins?

If you have a headache, you might take an aspirin to get rid of the pain. Aspirins have many brand names, but the tablets themselves are all made of the same chemical – acetylsalicylic acid. So what do aspirins do?

A headache is caused by something – tension, hunger, some sort of fever, a bad tooth, or something else. What aspirin, or any other painkiller will *not* do is to remove the cause of the headache. But what it will do is what doctors call 'raising the pain threshold'. This means that although the pain is still there, we cannot feel it. This is only temporary – as soon as the effects of the aspirin have worn off, the pain threshold drops again, and the pain will return. Aspirins should not be taken continually. If a pain returns repeatedly, then you should see your doctor. But if the headache vanishes, then you can be reasonably sure that the cause for your headache has gone, as well as the pain.

What is fallout?

Fallout is radioactive dust caused by the explosion of an atomic or hydrogen bomb. This dust can take years to fall back to earth after the explosion and can be very dangerous when it does. If it gets inside your body, by way of food or drink, it can damage the cells or weaken your body against disease, because its radioactive atoms break down and give off bursts of energy and matter that harm living cells.

Who were the Barbarians?

This was a word invented by the ancient Greeks to describe anyone who was not one of them! This even applied to the Romans, but the word was used by the Romans to mean any savage or uncivilised person, for example the Goths, Visigoths, Ostrogoths and Vandal tribes of the Dark Ages.

What did Peter Minuit buy on 4th May 1626?

The Dutchman gave a group of Indians beads, trinkets and cloth and in exchange got an island 14 miles (22km) long which lies between the Hudson and East Rivers. Today it is known as Manhattan Island and on and around it stretches the largest city in the United States – New York. Quite a bargain!

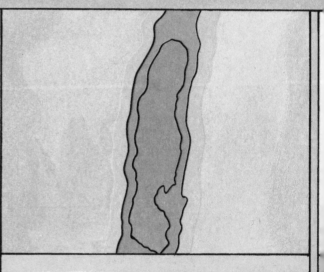

Why is the Dead Sea so called?

The Dead Sea is a long, narrow lake lying between Israel and Jordan in a deep trough in the earth's surface. In fact, it is the lowest area of water in the world, about 1,300ft (396m) below sea level. The River Jordan and other smaller streams drain into it, but not out again, so that any excess water evaporates away, leaving enormous deposits of minerals in the remaining water. The Dead Sea in fact is so salty that nothing can live in it – hence the name.

Which bird spends some time in prison?

The Great Indian Hornbill nests in hollow trees, perhaps using the deserted hole of a woodpecker. When the female has chosen a suitable spot, she and the male wall her up inside the tree, using a plaster made of mud, sticks, rotten wood and saliva. A small hole is left, just large enough for the male to pass food through to his mate. And here she will stay for up to two months, until her eggs are incubated and hatched, and the fledglings are able to fly away. Imagine how *you* would feel after being locked up with several screaming babies for that length of time!

Why do leaves change color in autumn?

How do homing pigeons find their way home?

This is not an easy question to answer, but it is generally believed that pigeons and other migrating birds have a sort of built-in clock-cum-compass in their brains that not only tells them when to migrate, but also which direction to fly, when to come back and how to get there.

The green color in all plants is caused by a substance called chlorophyll, which is manufactured by deciduous trees in the warmer weather of spring and summer. In autumn, the tree stops making it and so the green color vanishes, the leaves of the trees becoming the rich autumn colors we know.

How long does it take the sun's rays to reach earth?

It takes just eight minutes for the sun's rays to travel 93 million miles across space!

How was the Mediterranean Sea formed?

Six million years ago, the Mediterranean Sea dried up, leaving a lifeless desert 10,000 feet below the level of the Atlantic ocean. There were salt lakes in this desert, rather like the Dead Sea is today. Then, after a million and a half years, the Atlantic broke through the Straits of Gibraltar like a huge waterfall, flooding the basin to its present level. Scientists estimate that the filling up of the sea to the level we know today took about a hundred years.

Who was the first man on the Moon?

Not only the first man on the moon, but the first human being to set foot on alien land was Neil Armstrong, of the American Apollo 11 crew, who took that great step for mankind on 20 July 1969, and who was followed by Edwin Aldrin.

Where was the world's first subway built?

This was in London, and it was opened in 1863. Today's subway trains are electric, but the first ones were powered by steam, so you can imagine what a dirty way it must have been to travel!

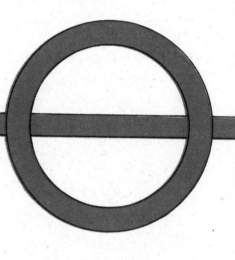

Where is the world's oldest university?

Not in Oxford or Cambridge, but in Fez, Morocco. Fez university has been open since AD 859!

What is the oldest newspaper in the world?

This honor goes to the Swedish *Post och Inrikes Tidningar*, which was founded in 1644.

What is the oldest locomotive still in existence?

The old railway engine is called 'Puffing Billy', and was designed by William Hedley. It was built in 1813, and can be seen today in the Science Museum, London.

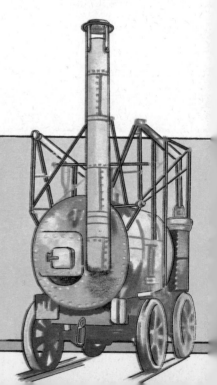

What is the world's largest sculpture?

In the Black Hills of Dakota in America there is a mountain called Mount Rushmore, and carved into the side of it are the heads of four of the greatest presidents of the United States — George Washington, Abraham Lincoln, Thomas Jefferson and Theodore Roosevelt. Each head is 60 feet (18 meters) high, and can be seen from a distance of 60 miles (96 kilometers) with the naked eye, and if the bodies of the four presidents had been carved too, the sculpture would have been 465 feet (142 meters) high.

Who did Captain Woodes Rogers meet on 31st January 1709?

Captain Rogers landed on Juan Fernandez Island in the Pacific Ocean — and was confronted by Alexander Selkirk, a Scot who had lived alone on the deserted island for four years, after quarrelling with his captain and being put ashore with only a few meagre provisions. Later, the author Daniel Defoe wrote a book based on Selkirk's adventures — *Robinson Crusoe.*

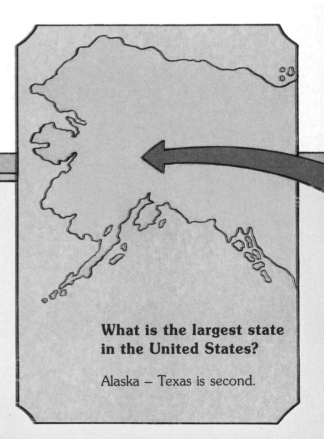

What is the largest state in the United States?

Alaska — Texas is second.

What is a kangaroo's tail for?

Kangaroos use their strong, thick tails almost as built-in stools, to rest against. The kangaroo's tail also helps it to balance when it makes long leaps and jumps.

What are freckles?

Skin pigment, or *melanin,* determines skin colour. Some people have melanin that is grouped in small areas of the skin, instead of being evenly distributed. Freckles are patches of melanin.

What are cows' tails for?

You have probably noticed that cows flick and turn their tails almost all the time, particularly in hot weather. It's what cows' tails are for — built-in fly swatters!

What is a rainbow?

We are only able to see rainbows in certain weather conditions: it must be sunny, but the sun must not be at its height, so mornings or evenings are best; and we must stand with our backs to the sun. When sunlight, which is white, enters raindrops, the drops act as *prisms,* and split the sunlight into its component colors: violet, indigo, blue, green, yellow, orange and red. So although we usually see sunlight as white, it is really made up of seven colors.

Do our bodies need salt?

Yes they do. Body cells must have salt in order to function, and as salt is lost continually it must be replaced. Salt has always been valued. Julius Caesar paid his soldiers in salt

Why do turtles live so long?

Turtles live longer than any other creature — often more than 200 years. They live so long because they do everything so slowly. They take about a year to hatch from eggs, and this sets the pace for their lives. They eat slowly, move slowly, grow slowly — even breathe slowly. During the winter hibernation period the turtle slows down even more.

What is an aqueduct?

An aqueduct is a man-made channel, often raised above the ground, for carrying water — usually a river or canal. The ancient Romans were excellent builders of aqueducts, and there are many to be seen still, especially in the southern regions of France. Rome itself was supplied with water by nine aqueducts with a total length of over 386 kilometres.

How did Sally Ride gain fame?

She was the first American female astronaut. She first flew in space in 1983.

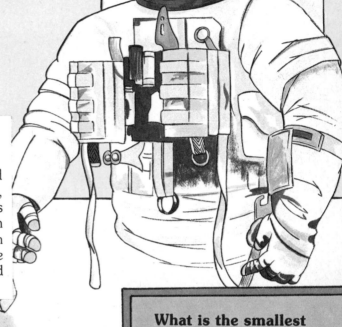

Who re-discovered the site of the ancient city of Troy?

Heinrich Schliemann had one ambition: to find the site of Troy. To this end he learned Greek, studied archaeology, and used Homer's *Odyssey* (which tells of the burning of Troy in the 12th century BC) to guide him. His search led to Hissarlik in Asia Minor, where in 1873 he found evidence of a burned city with fortified walls — Troy.

What is the smallest bird in the world?

The Bee Hummingbird, which is found in Cuba. It measures just 2¼in (5.5cm) beak to tail, though the female is slightly larger. It is illustrated here actual size.

Why was the Great Wall of China built?

It was built as defence against China's enemies, nomad warriors who came from the north. It was built in the 200s BC by Emperor Shih Huang Ti and was a great feat of building, taking hundreds of thousands of workers ten years to build. It was built by hand, with walls of brick and stone filled with earth. At the base the wall is some 25 ft (8m) thick, tapering to a minimum of 15 ft (5m) at the top, and the wall is about 25 ft (8m) high. Measured flat on a map the wall is some 1700 miles (2735km) in length, but it crosses high mountains and deep valleys and its actual length is estimated at 3000 miles (4827km). It is the longest fortified wall ever built, and in China is known as The Wall of Ten Thousand Li. (Li is a Chinese measurement of about ⅓ mile (.5km).

What was the Boston Tea Party?

It wasn't a party at all! A tax on tea was imposed in America by the then ruling British government, and this and other taxes were a big grievance. On 16 December 1773 after a political meeting in Boston, Massachusetts, about a hundred men dressed up as Red Indians boarded ships in the harbor which were carrying British tea. They threw the tea into the harbor waters, an act which became known as the Boston Tea Party and was one of the first actions against the British government. The Americans achieved their independence by waging a war against the British, which ended in 1783.

What are truffles?

Truffles are considered a very great delicacy in some countries, and people are prepared to pay a lot of money for one. They are a sort of edible fungus which grows underground in woody areas. Pigs are useful in finding them, and dogs too are used, as their superior sense of smell gives them the advantage over humans.

How long have we had women doctors?

In Europe there have been women doctors for only a very short time – since the last quarter of the nineteenth century, in fact. But in Egypt there were women doctors working two thousand years before the birth of Christ!

When was wine first produced?

Paintings in the tombs of Ancient Egypt dating from about 4500 BC show men and women gathering grapes and treading them in large troughs. Wine-making actually began some 10,000 years ago.

What was the Black Death?

In 1348 a great plague hit the world, spreading from China through all the countries of the east to Europe. The plague was called bubonic plague, and there were three different forms of it, all of which were very dangerous. It was also very contagious – so contagious in fact that historians believe that over a third of the population of Europe was killed by it. Since then, the plague has broken out in much smaller areas. The last big outbreak of it was in 1665 in London, England, when 68,000 people died. The plague was stopped a year later by the Great Fire of London, which got rid of the unsanitary conditions in which the plague bacteria had spread so quickly.

What is quicksand?

Quicksand is formed by a thick paste of sand and water floating on top of clay, and it is usually found at the seashore or at the mouths of rivers. Because the clay allows very little water to escape, the quicksand cannot drain, and it is very easy for objects to sink down into it. In fact, in 1875 an entire train sank into a huge patch of quicksand in Colorado, USA, and though probes were sent down to a depth of fifty feet (15 meters), nothing was ever seen of it again.

Are snakes slimy?

No, they are not. This is one of the most common mistakes people make about snakes. If you are lucky enough to get close to a non-poisonous snake, run your finger gently along it, and you'll find that it is in fact dry and smooth, not slimy at all.

How much does an elephant eat?

When kept in captivity, the elephant's diet can be closely monitored. In a week an adult will eat about 130lbs (60 kg) of food, one quarter of which will be hay, the other three quarters potatoes, cabbages, fruit, oats and dog biscuits. It will drink 15 gallons (68 litres) of water every day.

Do all bees make honey?

Yes, they all make a sort of honey on which they live – but only the honeybee makes honey that humans can eat.

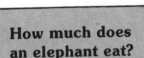

Can all birds fly?

No, there are a number of flightless birds. The penguin cannot fly, and is clumsy on land, but is a superb, fast swimmer. Even faster is the ostrich, the fastest land bird in the world. Other flightless birds include the kiwi from New Zealand, the emu and the cassowary from Australia, and the South American rhea.

Why do geese fly in formation?

Geese flying south in a V-shaped formation is a common sight. But why do they fly this way? On their long flights the geese follow a leader, an old, experienced gander who knows the way perfectly. If he flies at the head of the V, all the others can see and follow him easily. Planes flying in groups copy the geese, so that they can all see the plane in front of them.

How fast do an insect's wings beat?

Very fast! The bee's wings vibrate about 26,400 times a minute (440 times a second) but a tiny midge holds the wing-beating world record. It is able to beat its wings 57,000 times a minute – 950 times a second!

What is amber?

If you've seen amber jewellery in shops, you might think it's some sort of stone, like opal, but it's not. In fact, it's the remains of trees that lived millions of years ago. To be more accurate, amber is fossilised sap, crushed in the earth until it became hard. Sometimes amber is found which has insects trapped in it – they got in when the amber was still liquid millions of years ago and were trapped when it hardened.

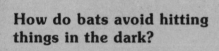

How do bats avoid hitting things in the dark?

Bats are remarkable creatures, not least because of their amazing radar system. They are nocturnal creatures, which means that they tend to be active only at night, but yet they never seem to fly straight into things. This is because bats give out very high-pitched squeaks, which bounce back off solid objects like walls and trees, so that the bats can hear the echo and move swiftly to avoid the obstacle.

Who invented the parachute?

The parachute is probably the oldest idea for a craft capable of carrying man through the air, and it is very simple: just a big umbrella that creates air resistance and so travels to earth slowly enough for the person wearing it to escape injury. Leonardo da Vinci sketched a parachute in 1514, but it wasn't until 1793 that a Frenchman called J P Blanchard claimed to have descended from a balloon by parachute, breaking his leg in the process.

What was a sedan chair?

In the 17th and 18th centuries, the sedan chair was a very popular way for people to be taken from place to place. It was a covered chair designed to carry one person at a time, and was carried by two men, one at the front and one at the back, holding it up from the ground with two long poles. This must have been tiring for the bearers, but very convenient for the passenger, since the chair had windows on either side and a top that could be raised to allow him or her to stand up.

How did America get its name?

Although Christopher Columbus was the first person generally believed to have discovered the New World, it was an Italian sailor called Amerigo Vespucci who actually discovered what is now called America. Columbus believed that the land he had found was in fact Asia, but Vespucci realised that it was not, and so in 1507 it was decided that the new land should be called after him.

What is the wettest place on earth?

Based on average yearly rainfall, the wettest place on earth is the island of Kauai in Hawaii, which averages about 460 inches of rain a year, or just over 11 meters! Good weather if you're a duck . . .

Who was Persephone?

She was the daughter of Ceres, the goddess of living things, and was kidnapped by the god of the Underworld. While she was in his kingdom, she ate only six pomegranate seeds, which meant that she had to stay there for six months of every year, returning to her mother for the other six. During her absence, Ceres forbids everything to grow, giving us winter, but on Persephone's return spring and summer come with her.

What is the lightest known metal?

Lithium. It is quite rare, and a soft metal, used mainly in the manufacture of stainless steel.

What is the largest diamond?

The biggest diamond ever found is the Cullinan diamond, now a part of the British crown jewels. When it was mined, it weighed 3106 carats.

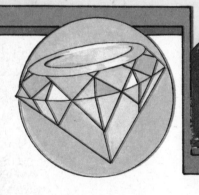

How much is a million?

A million is 10 times 10 times 10 times 10 times 10 times 10 – or 1,000,000. But how many is that? If you tried to count to a million at the rate of one number each second it would take you 11 days, 13 hours, 46 minutes and 40 seconds – without eating, sleeping or stopping!

What did Russia sell to America for 7,200,000 dollars?

Alaska! The land once belonged to Russia, but it was 8,000 miles from Moscow, and difficult to govern, so the Russians decided to sell to America. The deal was sealed in 1867 and in 1958 Alaska became the 49th state of the United States.

Who was Dick Turpin?

Dick Turpin was a famous English highwayman who began his life of crime as a boy, stealing cattle. Later he joined a band of smugglers, then he became famous for holding up coaches and robbing their passengers. He was hanged at York for horse-stealing in 1739.

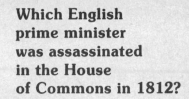

Which English prime minister was assassinated in the House of Commons in 1812?

His name was Spencer Perceval, and he was killed by John Bellingham.

Who was Anne Bonney?

She was something quite unusual – a female pirate. Though heiress to a large fortune she preferred to live the life of a pirate on the high seas.

The oldest person mentioned in the Bible lived for 969 years. Who was he?

Methuselah, the grandfather of Noah.

Who were the Four Horsemen of the Apocalypse?

They are described by St John in the Bible (Revelations) as representing four major kinds of disaster.

What is the oldest song in the world?

The oldest song ever recorded is the *shadouf chant*, which has been sung by irrigation workers on the Nile water mills ever since history was recorded – and that's a long, long time!

When does a Leap Year baby celebrate his birthday?

A baby born on February 29th will not have another actual birthday until four years later, when the next Leap Year occurs. So though a girl is twenty years old, she will only have had six 'real' birthdays. Leap year babies usually celebrate their 'missing' birthdays on February 28th or March 1st.

What is the best-selling book of all time?

The Bible.

What is a fresco?

A fresco is a type of wall-painting, derived from an Italian word meaning fresh. This is because the paint is applied on plaster while the plaster is still wet. As the plaster dries, so does the paint, and the picture becomes part of the wall.

What is special about British postage stamps?

Take a look at someone's stamp collection. All the foreign stamps may be very interesting to look at, but they all have one thing in common. Now take a look at a British stamp. Can you see what's different about it? It's all in the name – every other country in the world has it name printed on its stamps, except Great Britain, which incidentally was the first country to have stamps at all.

How do stalactites and stalagmites form?

Stalagmites look like icicles rising from the floor of caves, while stalactites hang from the roof. They are formed when water containing minerals called *calcites* drips through rocks in the cave roof. The water evaporates, either as the drip is hanging from the ceiling, or as it touches the floor, and large columns are built up from the minerals that remain. These are stalactites and stalagmites.

What is an extinct volcano?

A volcano is said to be extinct when it stops throwing out lava and stones, and also stops creating smoke and sulphurous gases. There are many volcanoes like this in the world, which are quiet and have been so for thousands of years, but it is by no means unknown for a volcano like this suddenly to erupt with devastating ferocity. The eruption of Vesuvius in AD 79 was an example of this – the inhabitants of Pompeii believed that it was dead.

What do tonsils do?

Tonsils are bundles of *lymphoid tissue* found at the back of the throat just behind the tongue. They are the first place that bacteria reach when they are inhaled or taken in by the mouth, and as such the tonsils are very easily infected by the very bacteria they are trying to get rid of. When they are infected, the tonsils swell, and become inflamed – this is called *tonsillitis* and if it is very severe, the tonsils can be removed.

What is the longest snake in the world?

Some snakes can reach extraordinary lengths, while others are tiny, and some reach an average length of about 5 ft (1.5 meters). The biggest snake recorded is the Reticulated Python of Asia, which often exceeds 20 ft (6 meters), and sometimes reaches lengths of 35 ft (10 meters).

What causes an earthquake?

The earth's crust is made up of several *plates* of rock, which move against each other very slowly. Where these plates meet is usually a danger zone, liable to have earthquakes – there is one very large danger zone along the coastline of California, USA, called the San Andreas Fault. When an earthquake happens, it is the result of the two plates slipping suddenly against one another along the line of the fault, and this sets up the most frightening and damaging tremors, causing very great damage.

What makes a wind?

Easy! Wind is the movement of air over the earth. When there is a rise in the earth's temperature, the air above it is heated and rises. Cooler air rushes in underneath the warm air to fill the space, and this cool air is what we know as wind.

Why do the oxpecker and the buffalo live in partnership?

The buffalo, which roams the African plains, always welcomes the attentions of a small bird called the oxpecker. The buffalo is always infested with small parasites which burrow into its hide; the oxpecker feeds on insects, and it pecks out the insects. Thus the buffalo helps the oxpecker by providing food, and the oxpecker relieves the irritation for the buffalo.

What is the world's deepest lake?

Lake Baikel in Central Asia.

What are taste buds?

Taste buds enable us to taste different flavours. On your tongue you'll see little lumps. Inside each lump are about ten or twelve taste buds. Groups of taste buds detect different tastes; areas on your tongue therefore register sweet, salty, sour or bitter tastes. Chemicals in the mouth alert the buds to carry messages to the brain, where tastes are identified. There are some 3,000 taste buds on the tongue.

Which planet is furthest from the earth?

Pluto, which is a staggering 2.671 billion miles away.

What is Halley's Comet?

In 1682 the then Astronomer Royal of Britain, Edmond Halley, was watching a comet pass the earth. This comet had been recorded several times before, at intervals of 76 years, and it had even appeared on the Bayeux Tapestry, which told the story of the Norman Conquest of England in 1066. Halley studied the comet intently, giving valuable information about it to posterity, and so it is now called after him.

What was the Pharos of Alexandria?

The Pharos was a huge lighthouse at the port of the Egyptian city of Alexandria. It was built of white marble, and stood over 133 yards or 120 meters high, with a beam that could be seen for a distance of over 20 miles (32 km). Eventually the Pharos was destroyed by an earthquake in the eighth century, but before that it was one of the Seven Wonders of the World.

Who was King Canute?

Canute was a Viking from Denmark, who came over to England with his army, defeated the old king, Ethelred the Unready, and himself took the throne. He ruled from 1016 to 1035, and was by all accounts a good king, much better than his predecessor, whose dithering cost him the crown. But what about the story of Canute trying to stop the sea from wetting his feet? Well, almost certainly this is not true — but if there was such an incident, it was likely to have been caused by the silly behavior of Canute's courtiers, who treated him as though he were a god. By showing them that he was not, Canute may have been giving them a lesson in Christianity — only God could stop the sea, and everyone else was only human!

Where is duelling legal?

In Uruguay — but only if both parties are registered blood donors!

Why do soldiers salute?

In the middle ages, knights wore helmets with visors — metal flaps over the eyes that could be raised or lowered. To see if another knight was a friend or an enemy, you put up your hand to raise the visor — and the hand movement was retained as a gesture of respect.

When was the earliest photograph taken?

The earliest photograph was taken in the summer of 1826 by a French physician and scientist, Joseph Nicephore Niepce. It showed the courtyard of his country house at Gras, and probably took about eight hours to expose.

What was the loudest noise ever heard?

In August 1883, the island of Krakatoa in the Pacific Ocean blew its top. A volcanic island, it had been rumbling for months. Then, suddenly, a mighty explosion took place. That bang was heard as far away as Japan; Australian lifeguards thought it was the rocket of a ship in distress and sent lifeboats out to help. Great tidal waves followed the explosion of the volcano, and some were even strong enough to reach Britain as abnormal swells. Scientists estimate that the force of the explosion was equal to that of about 3,000 atomic bombs, and the noise was the loudest ever heard on the earth. And what about Krakatoa itself? Well, most of the main island, where the volcano was, was blown skyhigh. All that remains is a huge submarine crater, and a few scattered islands.

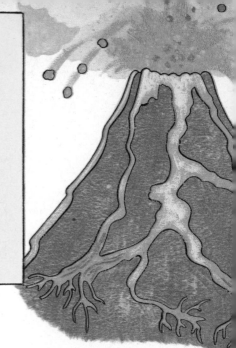

How old is the game of chess?

Chess is an extremely old game. It was probably invented in India over 1,500 years ago, although its name is derived from the Persian word *shah,* meaning king.

What is snuff?

Snuff-taking is a habit that was very common about two hundred years ago, and some people practise it still. Snuff itself is a form of powdered tobacco that is inhaled through the nose, and people can still have their own special recipes made up if they want to, although these days snuff is quite hard to find.

What is the Rosetta stone?

In 1798 the French invaded Egypt, and at a small town called Rosetta, a slab of black stone was discovered during building operations. On examining the stone, it was discovered that it bore an inscription in three languages – Greek and two forms of ancient Egyptian. This made it possible for scientists and historians to read the inscriptions on many ancient Egyptian tombs and monuments. Today the Rosetta stone is housed in the British Museum, London.

Was there really a Great Flood?

Scientists have recently discovered that there was indeed a great flood thousands of years ago – but it didn't engulf the whole world. Instead it flooded the land between the two rivers Tigris and Euphrates in Mesopotamia in the Middle East, which to the inhabitants *was* the whole world.

What are the Doldrums?

These are areas of the sea round the equator which have very little wind. Sailing ships took great care to avoid the Doldrums for fear of being becalmed.

How much rain falls on the earth in a year?

A lot! If the earth's total yearly rainfall fell all at once, the entire earth's surface would be flooded to a depth of three feet (one meter).

What is a Falabella?

The Falabella is the world's smallest breed of horse. Bred in Argentina, adults measure between 15–30in (38–74cm) at the shoulder, and weigh 40–80lb (18–36kg), no more than a large dog.

What are the solstices?

These are the two times of the year when the lengths of days and nights are of the greatest difference. In the Northern Hemisphere, the summer solstice is about 21st June, while the winter one is on or around 22nd December. In the Southern Hemisphere, of course, these are the other way round.

What was Pegasus?

Pegasus was the winged horse of Greek mythology, the mount of Bellerophon when he killed the fearsome, fire-breathing monster Chimaera. So brave was Pegasus that the gods made him into a constellation of stars when he died.

What is special about Przewalski's horse?

This strange-looking horse is in fact the only true wild horse still living in a natural habitat. It can be found in Mongolia, Asia, in small numbers, although some horses have been taken to zoos to ensure that the breed doesn't die out altogether.

Which fish blows itself up?

Not in the exploding sense exactly! The puffer is a tropical fish, which is sometimes eaten as a delicacy in Japan, despite the fact that some parts of its body are extremely poisonous. In the sea, a puffer lives up to its name, blowing itself up to twice its normal size to frighten away predators. It does this by taking in up to a litre and a half of water, which swells its belly like a balloon.

What is a boomslang?

A boomslang is a snake found in southern Africa – its name is Afrikaans for *tree snake*. The boomslang eats small reptiles, birds and mammals, killing its prey with its extremely powerful venom.

Why do people think that a cat has nine lives?

Thousands of years ago, the ancient Egyptians worshipped the cat as a god, and had a goddess called Pasht, who had a cat's head. The goddess was believed to have nine lives, and the belief was gradually applied to all cats. People still believe it today, which shows how long one superstition can last!

Why is the bowerbird so unusual?

To attract a mate, the male bowerbird of New Guinea makes a very elaborate *bower* or garden on the ground. Flowers, ferns, leaves and berries are often used, and when they wither, the bowerbird picks fresh ones.

Do fish drink?

Every living thing needs water, so all living things have to drink in one way or another. But when we see fish gulping in an aquarium they are not drinking: they are passing water over their gills, and extracting from it the oxygen they need to breathe.

Which insect lives the longest?

This honor belongs to the queen termite, which has been known to live for over fifty years. During this time she can lay over 30,000 eggs a day — so it is possible for her to lay half a billion altogether!

When were cats first domesticated?

We know that the Egyptians kept cats 4000 years ago; in fact, they worshipped cats as gods. When a house cat died, the whole Egyptian family (and their servants) went into deep mourning, and shaved their eyebrows off! The penalty for killing a cat was death.

What was the biggest hailstone ever?

The largest hailstone recorded was over seven inches (17 centimeters) across and weighed a pound and a half (675 g). Just imagine what might happen if something that size was to hit you on the head!

What are sunspots?

The sun can sometimes be seen to have dark spots on it which look a little like islands. They are in fact caused by gigantic electrical storms in the sun, and are believed to be large patches of gas, cooler than that around them. However, as we do not know of a way to get close enough to the sun, we cannot be sure.

How long does it take a stalactite to grow?

A very long time! Every centimeter of growth takes about 1,600 years!

What is a capybara?

The capybara is a rodent of tropical South America. It looks a little like a guinea pig, but grows to the size of a small dog, up to 4 ft (1.2 m) long, and about 100 lb (45 kg) in weight. It has webbed toes, and is a good swimmer.

What is fool's gold?

Many a prospector searching for gold has found what looks like a lump of the precious metal, only to discover that it is worthless. This mineral is easily mistaken for the real thing, because not only does it closely resemble gold, but it is also found where gold is found. In fact, fool's gold is a mineral called iron pyrite, which is not nearly as valuable as gold, and has led many a prospector to ruin!

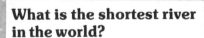

What is the shortest river in the world?

This honor belongs to the D River in Lincoln, Oregon, USA. It stretches for an incredible 146 yards (134 meters).

Where is the world's highest waterfall?

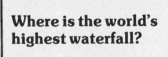

In Venezuela, South America. It is 3212 feet high (979 meters) and was found by an American pilot in 1935. The falls are named after Jimmy Angel, the pilot — Angel Falls.

Why do birds have beaks?

Bird beaks function as hand, tool and mouth. With them birds can collect nesting materials, build nests, find food and clean their plumage. They can even be used as a weapon. For example, the owl has a short, sharp, curved beak, ideal for ripping the flesh of the mice and other small creatures it preys on. The woodpecker, however, uses its straight beak like a chisel, picking insects from the trunks of trees, while ducks use their bills like sieves, taking in water and filtering out food.

What is a living fossil?

This term is used to describe animals that were thought to be extinct, but have been discovered alive. The coelacanth is one of these. In 1938 fishermen caught a coelacanth in the Indian Ocean, a strange looking fish, which had been known only as a fossil dating from 400 million years ago. This means that coelacanths were even older than dinosaurs – and were still alive; could someone find a living dinosaur one day?

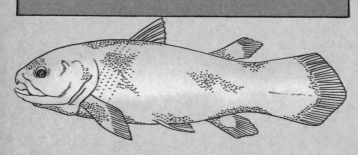

Is a sponge a plant or an animal?

Sponges look like plants, but they are in fact animals. They are one of the lowest forms of animal life. They do not move around, and have no sense organs, no reactions, and no heart, stomach or nerves. They are animals only in that they take in tiny plants and animals as food, digest them, and give off waste products.

Can dogs help deaf people?

We are familiar with dogs which help blind people lead an independent life, but now deaf people are also being helped. Dogs with very good hearing are trained to respond to sounds like phones and door bells by attracting their deaf owners' attention.

Why are flamingoes pink?

Flamingoes get their pink colour from the red-pink colouring matter in a type of shrimp that forms the basis of their diet. Flamingoes kept in zoos lose their pink colour if the pink shrimps are not included in their diet, so a harmless pink dye is added to their food.

Why does the Manx cat have no tail?

Nobody really knows, but legend has it that at the time of the Great Flood the Manx cat was so late in getting to the Ark that Noah closed the door before it was properly inside, cutting off its tail!

How can we tell how old a tree is?

Each spring and summer a tree adds new layers of wood to its trunk. Wood formed in spring grows fast, and is light in colour, because it consists of large cells. Wood formed in summer grows more slowly and is darker, because it consists of smaller cells. When the tree is cut these growth layers appear as alternate layers of dark and lighter wood. By counting the rings we can tell how old the tree is.

Who started the first zoo?

Although rich people have kept their own private collections of animals for thousands of years, it wasn't until 1793 that the first public zoo was opened. This was the Jardin des Plantes in Paris. These days, there are zoos in many of the world's cities.

What is a hill figure?

A hill figure is a carving of a human or animal shape in a hillside, so that it can be seen from a distance of several miles. There are a number of these figures, especially in Britain, the oldest being the Uffington White Horse in Oxfordshire. The horse was carved in chalk, so that it can clearly be seen, and it dates back to the late Iron Age, or about 150 BC.

How can you tell butterflies from moths?

Well, there are several differences, although not all of them are obvious straight away. Butterflies usually can be seen during the day, while moths prefer the night, and if you manage to get close to one, see if you can spot the blunt tips on the ends of the butterfly's antennae. The moth has branched or feathery antennae. Finally, if you spot a moth at rest, it will probably have its wings folded flat across its body. A butterfly will rest with its wings pointing upwards.

How does an echo sounder on a ship work?

An echo sounder simply measures the time it takes for an echo to reach an object and bounce back. For instance, if you were in a cave and you spoke, you could work out the distance to the far wall by the echo it makes. Knowing the speed at which sound travels, you could measure the time it takes for the sound to reach the far wall and bounce back, and thus work out the distance to the wall. This is what the echo sounder on a ship does. It was developed during the Second World War to detect submarines, but is now used as an aid to mapping the sea bed, and to locate fish.

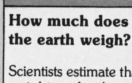

Which of the Seven Wonders of the World can still be seen today?

The Pyramids of Egypt, the oldest of the wonders, dating from about 2700–2300 BC. The most famous are the three Great Pyramids at Giza. It took some 100,000 men twenty years to build the largest one.

How much does the earth weigh?

Scientists estimate that the total weight of the earth is 6,600,000,000,000,000,000,000 tons, and it is increasing year by year due to meteoric matter from space settling on its surface.

Who was Wilson Bentley?

Wilson Bentley was an American whose great interest was snowflakes. As he grew older, he developed the technique of photographing perfect snowflakes before they melted. It was Wilson Bentley who discovered that no two snowflakes are alike.

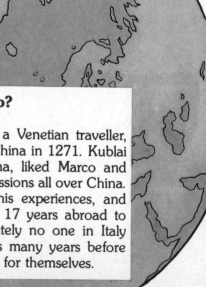

Who was Marco Polo?

Marco Polo, the son of a Venetian traveller, went with his father to China in 1271. Kublai Khan, the ruler of China, liked Marco and began to send him on missions all over China. Marco wrote down all his experiences, and returned to Venice after 17 years abroad to write a book. Unfortunately no one in Italy believed him, and it was many years before people discovered China for themselves.

What was the Riddle of the Sphinx?

The Sphinx was a terrifying winged creature, half woman, half lion, which asked travellers a riddle as they passed her. If they could not answer it, they were devoured by her. Only the Greek Oedipus knew the answer to the riddle, which was, "What is it that walks on four feet in the morning, two feet at noon, and three feet in the evening?" The answer is "Man", who crawls as a baby (four feet), walks upright as an adult (two feet), and uses a stick as an old man (three feet). The sphinx was so furious at being beaten that she threw herself off her cliff and died. There is a model of the Sphinx at Giza, by the side of the Great Pyramid, and millions of people visit it every year.

Which king of England married the most?

Everyone's heard of Henry VIII and his six wives, haven't they? The wives were Katherine of Aragon, Anne Boleyn, Jane Seymour, Anne of Cleves, Katherine Howard and Katherine Parr. And what happened to them? There's a useful rhyme that helps us remember –

Divorced, beheaded, died,
Divorced, beheaded, survived.

What is a centaur?

A centaur is an animal of Greek mythology with the head and torso of a man and the body and legs of a horse. Centaurs were said to be wild, fierce hunters, and are often depicted with bow and arrow. Look at a zodiac chart – Sagittarius, the archer, is depicted as a centaur.

How do escalators work?

The escalator or moving staircase is simply an endless belt moving around wheels. The stairs are attached to a central belt (or two side belts) which are driven by electricity. At the top and bottom of the escalator the steps fold flat, then travel under the escalator to the opposite end, where they open into steps again. Escalators run up or down; the direction in which the belt is driven determines which way.

When were buttons first used on clothing?

Buttons have been used to fasten clothing since ancient times. Archaeologists have unearthed buttons that date back 5 to 7,000 years, and were often made from gems, gold, or other precious metals. By the 1200s buttons were commonplace, used on the left side of garments for both men and women. During the Middle Ages men handling their swords found this inconvenient, so their buttons were changed to the right hand side, so that they could unbutton coats quickly with the left hand, and draw swords with the right. The custom of sewing men's buttons to the right side and women's to the left has persisted to modern times.

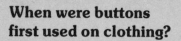

What was Mark Twain's real name?

Mark Twain was the pen-name of Samuel L. Clemens, the author of *Tom Sawyer* and *Huckleberry Finn*. Clemens used to work on the river Mississippi's paddle steamers, and got his pen-name from one of the cries of the boatmen – "by the mark, twain".

Who wrote a novel to pay for his mother's funeral?

English writer Samuel Johnson. The book was called *Rasselas*.

What is a black hole?

A black hole is a star which has collapsed in on itself, so that its gravity is immense and its weight incredible. So strong is the pull of its gravity that not even light and radio waves can escape it, and it is so dense that a matchbox-full would weigh 10 billion tons.

How many arms does a starfish have?

The answer is usually five – but it need not always be so. In fact, a starfish can have as many as forty arms, believe it or not!

What are the Dead Sea Scrolls?

In 1947, a boy was tending his father's goats in a rough and rocky area within sight of the Dead Sea. By chance, he found some old jars in a cave, and inside them were rolls of very thin leather with black markings on them.

These turned out to be the oldest manuscripts of the Old Testament of the Bible written in Hebrew. They were found to be about 2,000 years old, and other caves in the same area revealed more scrolls, amounting to the complete Old Testament except the book of Esther. This makes the scrolls priceless. By reading them in Hebrew, many scholars could settle arguments about the Old Testament that had raged for centuries, and those arguments are still being resolved today.

What is Ikebana?

Ikebana is the name given to the Japanese art of flower arranging, which is very different from the western idea of large flowery arrangements. Ikebana uses maybe one flowering spray, a few elegant twigs and some low greenery to create an impression of great grace, and each arrangement means something different.

When did the Olympic Games start?

The first games started thousands of years ago in ancient Greece. They were held every four years, as a religious festival honouring the supreme god Zeus. The modern games began again in 1896 in Athens. These too are held every four years, each time in a different city.

Who was Caligula?

Gaius, or Caligula as he was better known, was a Roman emperor. He was dismissed as mad by the historians of his time, who catalogued his follies and eccentricities. He considered himself 'one of the gods' and dressed accordingly; he also imported statues of the gods from Greece and had his own head carved on them! When his lavish entertaining threatened to deplete his wealth, he simply used his authority to revoke the wills of wealthy Romans and made their wealth payable to him. He thought up a grand plan to invade Britain. He marched a great army to the channel shore, then we are told that he 'told his troops to pick up seashells as trophies of war' and ordered them to turn back for Rome! Caligula even made his horse Incitatus a Roman consul!

What was the Black Death?

The worst epidemic known to mankind was the Black Death. In its most serious outbreak in 1347–51 a third of the population of Europe died.

The infectious organism was *Bacillus Pestis,* transmitted to man by fleas from the black rat. It caused a sudden onset of chills, fever, headaches and body pains, black or pink swellings known as *buboes,* madness and almost certain death.

On which side of a tree does moss grow?

Usually on the north side. This is because moss likes moist places and obviously there is least sunlight falling on the north side of a tree, making it darker and damper than the rest of the tree trunk.

Deep in a forest, however, where the rays of the sun cannot penetrate, moss may well grow on all sides of the trees.

Who originally spoke Latin?

Latin was originally spoken by people living in and around Rome, taking its name from one of the tribes living in the Tiber Valley, the *Latini.* The Latin that is used today comes from a period several hundred years later, by which time it had become a refined and dignified language used mainly by educated Romans, such as administrators, orators and writers. A more vulgar version was used by the uneducated masses.

Latin was the principal language of Europe for hundreds of years, and its influence on modern European languages is immense, although it has not been in general use itself since the Middle Ages. Latin is widely used for scientific and legal terminology.

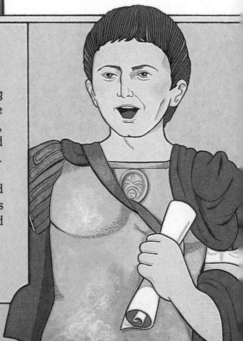

What is topiary?

Topiary is the art of cutting and training plants into ornamental shapes. Shrubs and evergreen trees are the plants most widely used and it is an art dating back to Roman times, when the geometrically minded Romans cut their trees into cubes, cones and pyramids. Later more ornate shapes became popular, especially in Europe in the seventeenth century when giraffes, dogs and peacocks made their appearance.

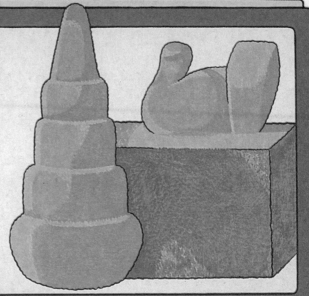

Why is sunshine good for you?

You know by instinct that the sun is good for you. But what exactly does it do to make you feel good? Well, it destroys certain fungi and bacteria on your skin, and also stimulates your white blood cells. These fight against illnesses to keep you healthy. Sunlight also 'recharges' your muscles and nervous system, wakes you up and gives you lots of energy. Last of all, sunshine creates an important vitamin in your body, vitamin D, the 'sunshine vitamin'. Too much sun, however, is harmful, so you must be careful not to have too much of a good thing!

When was the San Francisco earthquake?

San Francisco lies along the notorious San Andreas fault, a geological split in the earth's surface. At 5.15 am on 18th April 1906 the first of several massive tremors split streets and collapsed buildings throughout the city.

A giant tidal wave hit the waterfront, and fractured electricity cables and gas mains, starting fires which burned for three days. 25,000 buildings were lost, although miraculously less than 500 people died.

Why did the *Titanic* sink?

The *Titanic* was the largest and most luxurious liner of her time when she set out on her maiden, transatlantic voyage in April 1912 with 2,200 passengers and crew. Despite reports of icebergs in the vicinity, the *Titanic* maintained her speed of 22 knots and struck an iceberg which tore a 300-foot gash in her hull. Insufficient warning to abandon ship and inadequate lifeboat space meant that only 705 people survived.

How do flamingoes feed?

Flamingoes plunge their curved bills under water and sift water and mud through a fine, hair-like 'comb' along the edge of the bill, straining out the algae and shellfish on which they feed.

The lakes of Africa's great Rift Valley are home to millions of flamingoes. A million flamingoes on one lake will eat 65,000 tonnes of algae per year.

Why is Friday the thirteenth considered unlucky?

The number thirteen is supposed to be unlucky because there were thirteen people at the Last Supper, and Judas was the thirteenth guest. Another theory says that it's unlucky because there were twelve Scandinavian demigods until Loki, the evil one, made thirteen. Whatever the original cause of the belief, many people genuinely fear the thirteenth. Friday, too, is supposed to be unlucky. This was the day when Christ died, and the day when Adam and Eve ate the forbidden fruit. So when Friday and thirteen are put together, quite a few superstitious people feel that the day is unlucky.

Who created Sherlock Holmes?

Fiction's most famous detective was created by Sir Arthur Conan Doyle. Born in Edinburgh in 1859 he decided to become a doctor, and it was when he was studying medicine at university that he met the man who was to inspire him to create his most famous character. The man was his professor, Joseph Bell, who was particularly good at finding out not only what ailed his patients, but also through careful observation, details of their character, job and circumstances. It was his powers of deduction that so impressed Conan Doyle.

In 1887 Conan Doyle published his first Sherlock Holmes book, *A Study in Scarlet,* featuring the super-sleuth and his friend Dr Watson, and in the years that followed many other books and short stories appeared.

Although a successful writer, Conan Doyle continued to practise medicine, going to South Africa during the Boer War to treat injured troops, and he did some real-life sleuthing, too, championing those he believed had been wrongly convicted or badly treated. He was knighted in 1902.

What is an oscilloscope?

It is an electronic device which enables one to 'see sound'. Sounds are made by something vibrating, and so making the air around it vibrate. The motion of the vibrating object, back and forwards, compresses the air and then allows it to expand again, and this is repeated with each vibration. This in turn affects the air further from the object, such that the vibration travels through the air in all directions, until it eventually dies away. These vibrations are known as *sound waves,* and an oscilloscope shows the pattern, or shape, of these waves on a screen similar to a tv screen. The sound is fed into the machine through a microphone, which changes the energy of the sound waves into electrical energy, as an electric current.

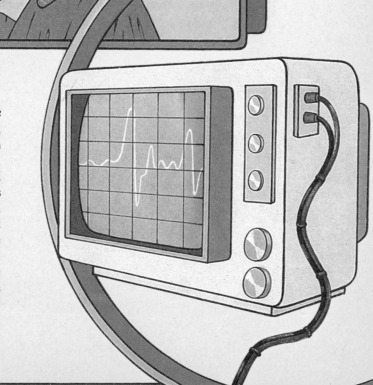

What are aphids?

Have you ever heard your parents complaining about greenfly on the roses or other plants in your garden? Well, the proper name for greenfly is aphids. They are insects, and can be very harmful to plants if they are not dealt with because they suck out the sap from the stem of the plant and make it grow stunted or deformed. They can also spread plant viruses, in particular one which attacks potato plants. But aphids have an interesting life style. When they have sucked out the sap from the plant, aphids secrete a sweet liquid called honeydew, which ants love. In fact, so fond are the ants of this honeydew that they keep herds of aphids near them, and they stroke the aphids' sides to encourage them to secrete the honeydew. A strange case of dairy farming in the insect world, isn't it?

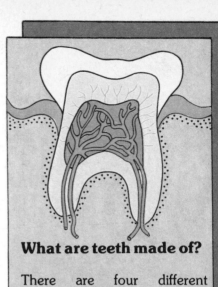

What are teeth made of?

There are four different substances which make up our teeth, and each substance has its own job to do. The hard and shiny white substance which covers every tooth is called *enamel*, and this protects the tooth from the bacteria which can cause decay. Lower down the tooth is a substance like bone which protects the root of the tooth. This is called *cementum*. Beneath the cementum is a material called *dentine*, which is a little like ivory, and which makes up the main body of the tooth. At the tooth's center is a space filled with dental *pulp*. This pulp contains the blood vessels and nerves that keep the tooth alive and cause it to hurt if bacteria manage to get through the two outer substances. This can be prevented if you take good care of your teeth, and there is every reason to do just that, isn't there? Who wants rotten and painful teeth?

Do sloths sleep all the time?

When we describe someone as being slothful, we mean that they are lazy and sleepy. But does the sloth really live up to this name? Is it as lazy as the term suggests? I'm afraid that the answer is yes, although it would be unfair to say that the sloth sleeps all the time.

The main characteristic of a sloth is that it does everything very, very slowly. In fact, it looks as if it is on film which has been slowed down until it has almost stopped. For example, the sloth moves about at less than half the speed of a human being walking slowly. And it does do an awful lot of sleeping! Out of every twenty-four hours, a sloth sleeps for nineteen. So idle is it that algae, greenish brown slimy plants, grow in its fur. Not a very endearing animal, is it?

What is a diamond?

Look in any jeweller's window, and you are bound to see diamonds, the white, glittering gems which are so valuable and so beautiful to look at. It's hard to think that the diamonds which sparkle in the shop windows came out of the ground as lumps of dull rock, isn't it? But this is how they are found.

Diamonds are made of the same element as the 'lead' in a pencil. This element is called carbon, but the diamond's carbon is in a different form. When rough diamonds are found, they look very uninteresting, just like ordinary stones, but the jeweller knows how to cut the stone so that it has many faces or *facets,* which catch the light and make the diamond sparkle. Diamonds are very valuable, not only for their beauty, but also for their hardness. They are the hardest known substance in the world. This means that they can be used for a wide variety of purposes in industry, but those which 'work' are called industrial diamonds, and are cut differently, making them not nearly as beautiful as the gem stones which go into rings and necklaces. Did you know that, because a diamond is so hard, it can only be cut with another diamond? No knife will do the job.

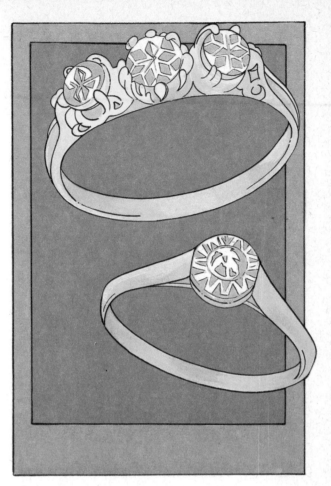

Why do we dream?

Nobody knows exactly *why* we dream when we sleep. All we know is that everyone dreams, although most dreams aren't vivid enough for us to remember them when we wake up. Dreams are not messages from other worlds, or prophecies of what may happen in the future, but very often the result of what we have been thinking about when we were awake, sometimes without us realising that we are thinking about it. For example, if we go to bed tired, cold or hungry, these feelings may well appear in our dreams. There is a tale about a man who went to bed hungry. He dreamed that he was eating a breakfast cereal, and when he woke up, he found that he had eaten some of his mattress! This is almost certainly not a true story, but it shows you an example of this link between our emotions and our dreams. We may also have dreams about the things we like best, or nightmares about the things we hate or fear. This is why many young children dream about fairies or witches, and why homesick people dream about their families or homes.

Why do muscles ache after exercise?

Whatever you do, you are using your muscles. Not all of them move at once — you have 639 muscles in all — but you would be surprised to know how many of your muscles you use doing something as simple as walking.

When your muscles are working, they produce an acid called lactic acid, which makes the muscles feel tired. When you rest, your body gets rid of the lactic acid, and you don't feel so tired. When you do a lot of hard exercise, like running a race, you may get cramp, a sharp pain in the muscles you are using the most. Cramp is caused by a big build up of lactic acid in these muscles, and a lot of rest is needed to get rid of the cramp. So although exercise, as we know, is good for your body, rest is just as good, and just as important.

What are amphibians?

Amphibians are creatures which can live both in the water and on land, and some examples of these are newts and salamanders, frogs and toads. In water, the amphibians can both walk and swim, but they tend to move quite slowly on land unless, like frogs, they can jump. Their skin is soft and damp, unlike snakes whose skin is dry and scaly, and they mostly have lungs instead of gills. To a certain extent, though, they can breathe through their skins, and some amphibians do have gills. Amphibians lay eggs — everyone has seen frog spawn, a blob of transparent, jelly-like balls with a black speck in the middle of each ball which will later become the tadpole. Toad spawn is in long strings like necklaces.

Who were the druids?

The druids were the priests of the Celtic people who lived in Britain before the Romans came. It is thought that these people arrived in Britain in 500 BC, when Stonehenge was itself a thousand years old. The druids worshipped trees such as the oak and the rowan, and especially the mistletoe, which was supposed to hold the life of the tree when in winter the tree appeared to die. It is doubtful whether the druids used Stonehenge as a temple as modern druids do today on Midsummer's Day. They preferred woods and other leafy places to worship in, and this made it extremely hard for the conquering Romans to find them and stamp out their religion. In fact they were never completely wiped out, the Romans deciding that it was better to tolerate them than to attempt the impossible task of getting rid of them altogether. Some of the druids' beliefs were similar to those of modern religions. They believed, for example, that the soul was immortal, and that on the death of the body, the soul passed to another body. But the method of entering their priesthood was very different from modern practices. Very strenuous feats had to be performed – for example, the candidate had to compose a long and complicated poem while standing up to his nose in icy water, as well as a whole series of other rites. We don't know how many druids there were at the time, but there are by no means as many today, despite a revival of interest in their cult.

What are fossils?

Fossils are the petrified remains of living things. There are three types of fossil, and each type is useful in telling us how creatures lived millions of years ago.

The first type of fossil is part of the body of the creature, usually the hard part of the body like the shell or the skeleton, which is preserved as it was originally. The second type is a mould of the creature's body, left in rock after the body itself has decayed, so that we can see exactly how the creature looked. The last type is the imprint of the animal's footprint in the clay or mud which has hardened into rock over the years. All these types of fossil are very useful for telling us what sort of animals lived on the earth millions of years ago, animals which have long since died out or changed slowly as time passed to adapt themselves to different conditions.

What was Alfred Nobel's achievement?

You've probably heard of the six famous Nobel prizes, awarded every year to the people who have made outstanding contributions to medicine, physics, chemistry, literature, economics and peace. Alfred Nobel was made famous because he invented dynamite in 1867. It seems a little odd, doesn't it? A peace prize bearing the name of the inventor of dynamite!

How much salt is there in the sea?

Every gallon of sea water has about four ounces of salt in it, on average. This means that if you dried the sea out to obtain the salt in it, there would be enough salt to put a layer of the chemical around the world 147 feet thick!

Who stole the British crown jewels?

You might think that nobody would have the skill or the courage to steal something as precious and easily recognisable as the crown jewels. But on 9 May, 1671, a daring Irishman, Colonel Thomas Blood, made a near successful attempt to steal them. Although he and his accomplices were caught and imprisoned in the Tower of London, they were not executed, as everyone had expected. Instead, the king, Charles II, was so impressed by the audacity of the robbers that he pardoned them, and even gave Colonel Blood a place at court and lands in Ireland!

Are all deserts hot?

The definition of a desert is a place where the lack of moisture makes it impossible for anything but a few special life forms to grow. This applies not only to hot places, like the Sahara and the Gobi deserts, but also to very cold places too. Because all or most of the moisture there is turned to ice, almost nothing can grow there, which makes it a desert. So, you see, a great deal of the Arctic is desert as well as the hot places people think of as being deserts.

Where does the term "in the chair" come from?

Long ago, only the very wealthiest people could afford a proper chair to sit in. Poorer folk used rough benches, stools or the floor. At meals, therefore, the lord or lady of the manor used the chair, while the less important people used the benches. At meetings today, the person who is in charge of keeping order is said to be *in the chair* or *chairing* the meeting.

Is the earth perfectly round?

No, it isn't. The earth is in fact like a rubber ball which has been gently squashed at the top and bottom, so that it is widest at the equator. It also has four bulges which form rough corners. These are in Ireland, and near the countries of Peru, South Africa and New Guinea. Scientists call the earth's shape an 'oblate spheroid'.

What does the skeleton do?

The skeleton does two very important jobs. It holds the body up, and it protects the delicate organs of the body. When a baby is born, it has about 270 bones in its body. These are small and quite soft, and as the child gets older some bones fuse together, so that there are about 206 by the time the child is fully grown. The skeleton has joints which enable it to move easily. The most flexible joints are the ones like that at the hip – these are called ball and socket joints. Other joints don't move at all – the skull is an example of this. Although it is made of many different bones, most of these don't move, the only one that does being the jaw bone. The skull protects the brain from injury, while the rib cage protects the heart and lungs, and the backbone (which is a long chain of small bones) protects the spinal cord, the 'main road' of the nervous system.

Why do we need vitamins?

First of all, what are vitamins? They are substances which are necessary to life, and they are produced by various plants and animals. Everybody must have these vitamins in their diet regularly to enable the body cells to grow and repair themselves. Although scientists have long and complicated names for vitamins, we know them best by their simple letters, A, B, C, D, E, and so on, and each one performs a vital job. Vitamin A, for example, helps prevent infection, and Vitamin C prevents scurvy, a disease which makes the body's bones weak and the teeth loose. Vitamin D is especially important for growing children as it makes their bones strong. If we have a good balanced diet, the chances are that we are getting all the vitamins we need.

Did dragons ever exist?

Dragons have always been very popular subjects for folklore and legends. There are friendly dragons, but most of them are very hostile and likely to kill on sight with a burst of flames from their nose or mouth. Almost every hero in folklore has killed a dragon at some point in his career, as well as all the other daring feats he is supposed to have performed. But what are dragons, and did they ever exist at all?

The answer is probably that the first stories of dragons sprang out of the discovery by ancient man of the huge fossilised bones of the dinosaurs. These men realised that the bones belonged to enormous lizards, and indeed if you look at old pictures of dragons they look very much like dinosaurs as we now know them to have been. No one knows the origin of the tales about fire breathing. It was probably added to make the hero's courage in killing the dragon seem even greater, although anyone who had the courage to approach a dragon like that, let alone kill it, would have been brave enough!

Where does vanilla come from?

Vanilla flavoring is something we are all familiar with. But did you know that we get vanilla from the vanilla orchid, which grows on Madagascar and other islands in the Indian Ocean? What is more, the vanilla orchid is the only orchid which produces a useful product.

How are clouds formed?

Clouds are formed when warm moist air rises into the sky. When it reaches a certain height, the warm air cools down and the water vapour in it condenses into small drops of water, forming clouds. There are several different types of cloud. The ones which are highest are usually made up of drops of ice, and are the thinnest. These are called *cirrostratus* and *cirrocumulus* clouds. Lower clouds are called *altostratus* and *altocumulus* clouds. Lower still are the *stratocumulus* clouds and the *nimbostratus* clouds – these are the thick and shapeless rain clouds – and the lowest of all are the *stratus* clouds, which are seen as fog over high, mountainous regions. Thunder clouds are called *cumulus* and *cumulonimbus* clouds, and these are the fat, cauliflower shaped ones.

Who was the real Robinson Crusoe?

Daniel Defoe's fictional hero Robinson Crusoe is well known today. But not so well known is the real castaway, a Scotsman named Alexander Selkirk, who chose to be left on Juan Fernandez, an island named after a Spaniard who had discovered it a hundred years earlier. After living there alone for over four years, Selkirk was found and rescued by a British ship and returned home to Britain, where his adventures inspired Defoe to write *Robinson Crusoe*.

How did the Oscar get its name?

In 1929, the first awards for best performances in films were made. These awards were shaped like a man, and a secretary at the Academy of Motion Picture Arts and Sciences, on seeing one for the first time, remarked that it looked just like her uncle Oscar. The name stuck, and the awards have been called Oscars ever since.

Where does cork come from?

Cork is the thick and spongy bark of the cork oak tree. These trees don't grow to be very tall, but they have quite thick trunks. Taking the cork bark off the tree can only be done every ten years, but about forty-five pounds, or about twenty-two kilograms of cork can be stripped off one tree at a time, so that every ten years a plantation of cork oaks can give a very high harvest.

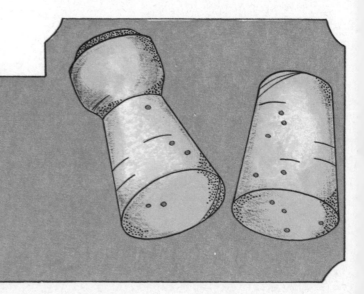

Why is lighting three cigarettes with one match said to be unlucky?

During World War One (1914–1918), soldiers fought in trenches, watching out for the enemy, who were never very far away, in *their* trenches. It was believed that striking a match at night and lighting three cigarettes with it, gave the enemy time to aim and fire at the match's light, and thus the soldiers themselves. So, lighting a third cigarette with the same match was not only unlucky, it was dangerous too.

Where do we get the word *denim* from?

If you have a pair of jeans, you will know that what they are made of is a cloth called denim, but do you know where the word comes from? At first, it was used to describe a serge cloth made in Nimes, France – the original name was '*serge de Nimes*'. Gradually, these last two names were shortened and adapted to the word we know as *denim*, although now denim is made all over the world and not just in Nimes.

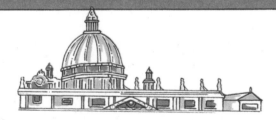

What is the smallest country in the world?

The smallest country in the world is the Vatican City, which is less than one square mile in area, and is completely surrounded by the city of Rome. The Vatican City has its own national anthem, stamps, newspaper and radio station, and has a population of just under a thousand people.

Why do birds migrate?

Not all birds migrate, but a lot of them do, two of the best known British migrating birds being the swallow and the house martin, which fly south in the autumn to spend the winter in parts of Africa. The reason they do this is because of the need for food, of which there is a great shortage in northern Europe during the winter – these birds eat mainly insects which die or hibernate in winter.

So why doesn't the swallow stay in Africa all year round? The reason is that it breeds in Europe rather than in Africa. This is also the case when fish such as salmon travel each year to places where they feed.

It isn't only European birds which fly south. North American birds fly south in the winter too. In the southern hemisphere, when winter takes place at the same time as European summer, Australian birds fly north to places like Malaysia to escape the winter. They are there from April to September, and between October and March Malaysia sees northern hemisphere birds like cuckoos and plovers arriving to spend the European winter months there too. So Malaysia has a regular colony of foreign birds at all times of the year. It makes you wonder what happens to all the native birds of Malaysia when all these visitors arrive, doesn't it? They must never have the place to themselves!

Is there life on other planets?

Not on any other planet in our solar system – the other planets are either too hot or too cold to support life as we know it. The only other planet which it was thought might possibly have had life on it was Mars, but recent space voyages have discovered that its atmosphere was not suitable to support life. However, when you consider all the other solar systems in the universe, where man has not yet explored, it seems very unlikely that no other planet has some form of life on it. Many people imagine aliens to be the same basic shape as humans, but this need not necessarily be the case, and that does not mean that they would necessarily look hideous. After all, aliens might be absolutely horrified by our shape, if they had never seen it before!

What does the appendix do?

Some people believe that the appendix 'catches' things like fruit pips, and has to be removed when it is full. This is not true. In fact the appendix does nothing at all, and we would manage very well without it.

So, what is the appendix? The appendix is a small tube at one end of the large intestine. It is closed at one end, like a sort of pocket. The appendix has to be removed when it becomes seriously inflamed by an infection, which is quite common. Substances from the intestine enter the appendix and cannot easily get out again. If they stay there, these substances may harden, forming a plug, which squeezes the appendix's blood vessels. This can cut off the blood supply to the appendix, and an infection may easily arise. Pain starts in the stomach, and then is concentrated on the right side of the body. Then it is a case of calling for the doctor and having the appendix removed by a simple and quick operation.

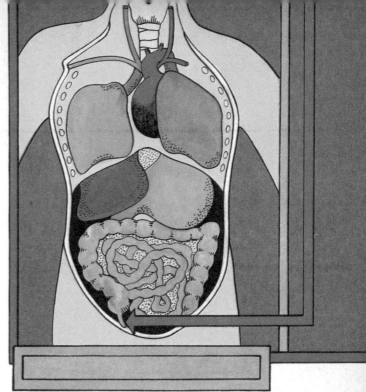

Who was Achilles?

You may have heard people saying that somebody has an 'Achilles heel', which means that they have a weak spot somewhere, either in their personality or their body. Where does that expression come from, and who was Achilles?

Achilles was the son of a woman called Thetis, who was told by the Fates, ancient Greek goddesses who controlled people's destiny, that her baby would die young. Thetis took the child and went to the river Styx, where she dipped the young Achilles into the water, which was supposed to make him impossible to wound. When she did this Thetis held her son by his heel, so that this part of his body was not protected as was the rest. Later, Achilles became one of the most famous of all Greek heroes, and was a warrior in the Trojan wars. During these wars, Achilles captured a girl named Briseis, who was taken away from him by the Greek leader Agamemnon. Achilles refused to fight any more for Agamemnon, but he lent his armour to his friend Patroclus, who led the Greek army in his place. The Trojan champion Hector killed Patroclus, and Achilles decided to seek revenge. He killed Hector and dragged his body round the tomb of Patroclus. Achilles was killed when Hector's brother Paris shot a poisoned arrow at him. It struck his heel, the part not protected by the water of the Styx, and Achilles died. The story of the Trojan wars was told by a Roman poet called Virgil, in a long poem called the *Aeneid,* and it makes very good reading if you can find a translation of it.

Why do we need salt?

We already know that the body contains a lot of water – in fact over 70% of the body is composed of water. But this isn't pure water. It is a salt solution, and as we lose a certain amount of our body fluid every day, we also lose salt, which we must replace. We don't get salt from vegetables and plant food, but we do get it from meat. This is why purely meat-eating animals don't need extra salt, whereas those who eat only vegetation, such as cows, do need extra salt. Because most people eat both vegetables and meat, we only add a very little amount of salt to our meals. If we had no salt at all in our diet, we would soon go mad for lack of it.

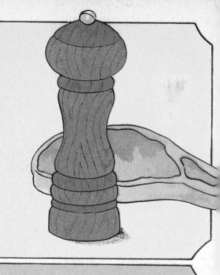

How do insects breathe?

Insects don't have lungs like you or me. Instead they have a tube system, which runs all over their body, and which carries air to all parts of the body. These tubes are called *trachea*. The air is carried to the body when the movement of the insect's muscles pumps it there through openings in the insect's skin.

How do we see?

The human eye is shaped like a ball with a bulge in the front. In the middle of this bulge is a hole called the *pupil*, which is the part we see as the black circle in the middle of the colored *iris*. The pupil lets in light to the eye. Behind it is the *lens*, which focuses the picture of what we can see. When light passes through the lens, it is turned upside down, so that an upside down picture is the image which hits the *retina*.

The retina is that part of the eye which actually makes sense of what we see. It is sensitive to light, and can sort out all the different colors we see. When light hits the cells of the retina, a chemical change takes place in the cells. This starts messages or impulses in the *optic nerve* at the back of the eye, which takes these messages to the brain. The brain turns the images the right way up, and identifies them as something we can recognise. Have you ever wondered why the pupils of the eyes grow bigger and smaller? This happens according to the amount of light available. In bright light, the pupil closes up to a black speck, letting through only enough light to be able to see without damaging the retina. When the light is very dim, the pupil opens up to let in as much light as possible, so that, again, we can see.

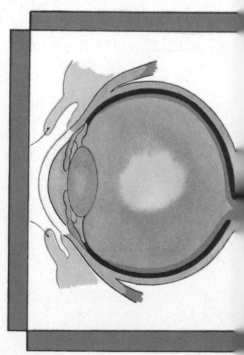

Why are some people left-handed?

When a person is left-handed, all it means is that they can do certain things better with the left side of their body than with the right. You may have noticed that some people write with their left hand instead of their right, and that they hold their knife in their left hand, and other similar things. This is not 'wrong', and in fact attempts to force someone to become right-handed can often do more harm than good. But what causes left-handedness? Nobody can really say. It is not something with a single explanation. One theory is that the human body is not the same on both sides – that is, it is not symmetrical. One side dominates the other, and it is believed that the two halves of the brain control this, the left side of the brain controlling the right side of the body, the right side of the brain controlling the left side of the body. In most people, the right side of the body (the left side of the brain) dominates, but in left-handed people the opposite is the case. But nobody knows why this should be so, and in any case, not all scientists accept this theory.

What is the sun?

When you look up into the sky on a clear night, you see lots of stars twinkling there. The sun is a star, and it shines by its own light, which is formed by bursts of energy from the inside of the sun rising to the surface. The sun is extremely hot – so hot that it would turn anything which got too close to it into gas, even something as solid as a piece of steel. We don't know very much about the sun, because of course we can't get close enough to it to do tests, as we have on the moon. But what we do know is that the sun is a very average sized star, and that it is not abnormally hot when compared to others. We also know that if the sun stopped shining, the earth would be destroyed because the sun's heat keeps everything alive. Fortunately it contains enough energy to carry on shining for billions of years to come.

Are there such things as fairies?

Do you believe in fairies? You have probably read lots of stories about them, but possibly you don't believe that they exist. Well, if you are doubtful about them, here's a story that may well interest you.

In 1917 two young girls in Yorkshire borrowed a simple camera and took some photographs – which still have to be explained. They showed the girls in a copse behind their houses, apparently playing with and talking to fairies, little people about the size of a hand, with wings and traditional elvish faces. Of course, everyone said that the pictures were fakes, and that the girls, Elsie Wright and Frances Griffiths, had somehow tricked everybody. But when it actually came to examining the pictures, the experts could find nothing to prove that the girls had tampered with anything on the camera or the film. It seemed that they really had taken pictures of fairies. Not content, the experts went to Yorkshire and gave Elsie and Frances a camera with specially marked film, and asked them to take some more photographs of the fairies. The girls did so, and the result was more pictures of the fairies. And still nobody could say that the photographs were anything but genuine. People have tried ever since to find something in the photographs which would prove that they were faked, but nobody has been able to do so, and the Yorkshire fairies have remained a mystery ever since.

What is a Dowser?

A dowser is another name for a water-diviner – someone who can tell where there is water lying underground. The dowser uses a whole variety of tools to find the water, but one of the most common is the Y-shaped twig from a hazel tree. The dowser holds the twig by the two prongs of the Y, with the long stem pointing upwards. When the twig is above a spot where there is water beneath the surface of the earth, the stem of the twig will suddenly dip downwards, or in some cases it will twist itself violently out of the hands of the dowser.

Nobody knows exactly how this is done, not even the dowsers themselves, but it may be that they have some special powers which the rest of us don't possess – it is certainly true that only a very few people can do this.

Who are the Pearly Kings and Queens?

In the 1880's a huge cargo of fashionable pearl buttons arrived in London from Japan. One of the street vendors in the markets of the time liked the look of them, and he decided to sew a few of these buttons around the hems of his trousers. The fashion soon caught on among the street vendors, with people trying to outdo one another in the number of buttons they had on their clothes and the various patterns they were in. The Pearly Kings and Queens were elected by the rest of the street vendors, or *costers* as they were known, to lead them against bullies who were trying to drive them out of their *patch*.

Today, the Pearlies are still in evidence in London, their clothes encrusted with pearl buttons sewn in various complex and detailed patterns and designs. These days, however, the pearly clothes are worn only for things like charity work and special occasions – they are much too heavy and ornate to work in!

Who was Dick Whittington?

If you have heard of Dick Whittington at all, then you'll probably know him as a fairytale character, with his cat, and the Bow Bells saying those famous words: "Turn again, Whittington, thrice Lord Mayor of London!"

Just a story? Well, not quite. Dick, or to give him his full name, Sir Richard Whittington, really did exist, although you can forget the story about the cat and Bow Bells. Dick was the son of a wealthy Gloucestershire landowner in the fourteenth century. He decided to try life in London, and soon became very successful and very rich. He built almshouses and libraries in the city, and restored Saint Bartholomew's Hospital, which is still in existence today. And yes, he did become Mayor of London three times. He was also a great favorite of the king, Edward the Third — though this may have been because of his wealth! Records show that Dick Whittington often lent the king money — but he didn't lose that friendship when it came to reclaiming the debt. Instead, the wise Mayor of London burned all the bills in front of the king himself, wiping out any money that he was owed and thus ensuring that he would continue to be in favor.

How do oysters make pearls?

Pearls are some of the most beautiful gems we know, and very expensive to buy. So it may come as something of a surprise to learn that pearls start off as irritating grains of sand and other substances which get into the soft part of the oyster. The oyster is a mollusc, which means that it has a soft and very sensitive body inside its hinged shell. When a grain of sand or grit gets inside the shell and on to the soft body of the oyster, the creature covers it with layer upon layer of a hard smooth substance called nacre, which is the same substance which makes mother-of-pearl. It does this to cut down the irritation caused by the sand, and it adds more and more nacre, forming the pearl. It is easy to see how people hit on the idea of deliberately putting a grain of sand or a small bead inside the oyster and allowing the animal to cover it with nacre, so that the oyster forms what is called a cultured pearl; although these are real pearls, they are started deliberately.

What are nerves?

Nerves are the organs which tell us what is going on in the world outside our bodies, and which take messages about this world to the brain, which translates the messages into feelings. There are four types of nerve in the body. The first is the one which picks up messages like pain, light, cold and heat. The second type of nerve receives these messages and sends others to parts of the body which cause swift action to be taken. For example, if you touch a hot iron, the first type of nerve tells you it is hot, and a split second later the second sort of nerve makes your muscles pull your hand away in what is called a reflex action. The third type of nerve takes messages over longer distances in the body, and is the type of nerve which makes our body do the things our brain orders it to do, such as moving parts of the body to perform certain actions. The final sort of nerve is that which transmits messages from the first type, called sensory nerves, to the brain where the messages are translated into feeling. This is why, having touched the iron, we may not feel the pain until just after we have pulled our hand away. We have nerves all over our body, although there are more in certain parts than in others. The central nervous system, through which all messages pass, is composed of the brain and the spinal cord, which is why we have to take special care not to damage our heads or backs.

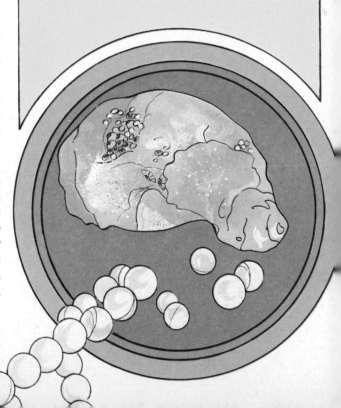

Who was Lady Godiva?

Long ago, in Anglo-Saxon times, the people of the town of Coventry, in England, were saved from paying very heavy taxes by the action of their countess Godiva, who rode naked round the town to prove to her husband, Earl Leofric, that she was ready to do almost anything to make her people's life easier. This is the legend, and in Coventry itself there are monuments to Lady Godiva, streets named after her, and even a clock which, every hour, re-enacts her ride. But who was the real Lady Godiva?

Godiva, or as she was probably called by her subjects, Godgifu, was a very wealthy landowner, and her prize possession was Coventry. She was married to Leofric, who was the Earl of Mercia, a big area covering all of the midlands and most of what is now the north of England. Both were Christians, and the ruins of a church they built in Coventry can still be seen. Legend has it that on her famous ride, Godiva asked the townspeople to go indoors and shut their doors and windows so that she would not be seen. She was disobeyed by a man who has become known as Peeping Tom, but he never saw her because he was struck blind by a divine light as he opened his window. Peeping Tom is a much later addition to the story, and probably did not exist at all. As to the question of Godiva's nakedness, many stories change over the years. One word changed for another with a slightly different meaning can make a great difference to a story, and it is more than likely that instead of riding naked, Godiva rode in Coventry without the usual badges of her rank as Countess of Mercia. She may also have ridden unattended, something which was never done in those violent times when Viking raids were still part of everyday life. The legend says that Leofric was so impressed by her goodness and trust in her people that he lowered the hated taxes, and Godiva has become a local heroine. We shall never know the exact truth of the story, because like so many other legends it was never written down, and merely passed on by word of mouth. But every child in Coventry knows the story, and even today, Lady Godiva is a heroine.

Did King Arthur ever exist?

Everyone has heard of King Arthur and his Knights of the Round Table, of Lancelot and Guinevere, and the quest for the Holy Grail. Many stories have been told about the court of Camelot ever since the Middle Ages, when such romantic tales were popular. But stories are all these legends are — it is very doubtful whether Arthur, the romantic hero of legend, ever did the deeds he was supposed to have done. However, it is certain that in the sixth century there was a chieftain, perhaps of Romano-British descent, who may have led his people in battles to defend Britain against Saxon invaders. This chieftain may have been Arthur, although he is only referred to in old writings as *Dux Bellorum*, a Latin title meaning war lord. Nobody knows where Arthur's capital city and palace of Camelot is, although many places all over Britain and in parts of France have claimed to be the site, and despite the lack of proof about Arthur's existence, stories about him and his knights are still very popular. A very well known tale is that the king did not actually die in his last battle of Camlann, but was carried away to Avalon (which might be another name for Glastonbury in Somerset) to sleep beneath the hills until his country needs him again in a time of great crisis.

What are thunder and lightning?

Some people become very frightened during a thunder storm, but there's really nothing to worry about. Lightning is the result of a collision between two electrical charges – one positive, and the other negative – either in two clouds or in a cloud and the earth. When the difference between the two charges becomes great enough, a great spark – the lightning – jumps between the two. Thunder is caused when that electricity has been discharged. The air expands and contracts rapidly, and the air currents collide violently, causing the rumbling noise we know as thunder. You may have heard stories of people and things being struck by lightning. The spark of electricity hits the earth and is absorbed by it. Sometimes it does hit things like trees, but the likelihood of it hitting a person is very small indeed, and there is no need to be frightened of a storm.

What causes different skin colors?

If you walk down a street in any town or city, you will see lots of people with different colored skin: white, black, yellow and coffee colors all appear. But why do people have different colored skin?

The reason is that in your skin you have substances which, under certain conditions and with the correct chemical processes, make colors — the different shades of human skin. The amount of each different color or *chromogen* in your skin determines what color you are. One of these colors is formed by a substance called *melanin*, which appears as black or dark brown when it comes into contact with sunlight, and which gives you a sun tan. Everyone has melanin in their skin, but people who live where the sun shines all year round have more melanin in their skins than people who live in colder areas. It protects them against the harmful rays of the sun. Other colors in the skin are yellow, which is caused by a similar process as black; red, which is caused by the presence of blood vessels in the skin, and white, which is the color of skin without any color in it. The balance of these four colors in your skin decides what color you are.

Why was King Alfred called 'the Great'?

Well, he was not called 'the Great' because he was a tall man; he was not. Alfred became king of Wessex (a small British kingdom including what is now Hampshire, Somerset and Wiltshire) in AD 871, at a time when the Vikings ruled over large parts of England. The king was determined to defeat the pagans, under their king, Guthrum, and he succeeded. By the time of his death in 899, almost all of England was under his rule, and the Viking armies were defeated in many battles. Alfred was a Christian, and when he was young he had been sent to Rome to be blessed by the Pope. But despite his faith Alfred, like most kings of his time, was proud of the fact that he was descended from pagan gods like Woden. There is one legend about Alfred which everyone knows – that while hiding in a woman's cottage in Athelney marshes, Somerset, at a time when the Vikings seemed to be winning, Alfred was supposed to be looking after some cakes, so that they did not burn. Thinking deeply about the state of his country, he forgot the cakes, and they burned. When she came back, the woman scolded him. Alfred apologised and paid for the cakes.

It is very doubtful whether this ever happened, but what it shows us is that people believed Alfred to be a kind and humble man, and we know that they willingly followed their brave and wise leader into battle against the invading Vikings.

Do fish sing?

Well, it's not exactly singing, but some fish can make musical sounds. The siren fish of the Mediterranean can make a tuneful noise by grating its teeth together, and the drumfish is so called because it can make a noise like a drum, so loud that fishermen sixty feet above it on the surface have heard it.

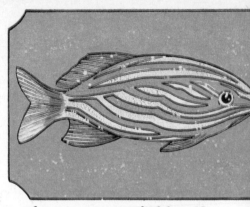

What color is an insect's blood?

Did you know that insects don't have red blood like us? Instead their blood is either colorless or a very faint green or yellow. If you manage to squash an insect, and you see red blood, you can be sure that that red has come from the blood of some animal the insect has bitten.

How fast can birds fly?

Quite amazingly fast! Even the common sparrow can reach fifty miles an hour, and the duck can reach seventy. But the speed record goes, not surprisingly, to the aptly named swift. This amazing bird can reach speeds of over a hundred and six miles an hour!

What fish swims standing up?

Did you know that the sea horse is the only true fish which swims in a standing up position, and not lying down as other fish do?

Is there an animal which has three eyes?

Surprisingly, there is. This is the tuatara, a reptile which looks like a lizard. In some lizards there is a gland at the front of the brain called a *pineal body,* shaped like an eye. In most of these lizards, the pineal body is not fully developed, and does nothing at all, but in the tuatara's case, it is developed fully, and acts as a third eye.

Do mice really like cheese best?

If you had seen nothing but cartoon strips, you might think so. But in reality, mice, like all rodents, prefer vegetables and grain to cheese, and will only eat it when they are very hungry.

Why is the animal called a pig, and its meat called pork?

This is because words like pig, cow, sheep and calf come from the Anglo-Saxon or Old English language. After the Norman conquest in 1066 the wealthy French-speaking landowners called these animals by their French names when they ate them, giving us the words pork, beef, mutton and veal. The Anglo-Saxons, however, carried on calling the animals by their original names, so we have both sets of words.

What is the most poisonous snake in the world?

This title belongs to the Australian tiger snake, which is only five feet long. Its poison glands contain enough venom to kill three hundred sheep!

Who was the Elephant Man?

'The Elephant Man' was a cruel name given to a man called Joseph Merrick, who was very severely deformed. Although he died before he was thirty years old, Joseph Merrick became a celebrity in Victorian England because, despite his deformities, he was a gentle, intelligent and brave man. When he was young, unscrupulous men exhibited him as a freak in fairs and circuses. Later he met Frederick Treves, a London surgeon, who treated him with respect and kindness and gave him a permanent home at the London Hospital. One of Merrick's greatest moments came when the Princess of Wales, later Queen Alexandra, visited him in the Hospital and talked to him for some time. He had always previously been regarded with horror because of his strange appearance.

What is Big Ben?

If you thought that the clock in the tower of the Houses of Parliament in London was called Big Ben, you would be wrong. The tower itself is called St Stephen's Tower, while the clock is called the Westminster clock, and it is the bell that strikes the hour which is called Big Ben. This bell weighs thirteen tons, so it is no wonder that it is called *Big* Ben!

What was the Trojan Horse?

The story of the Trojan Wars was told in a poem by the Greek poet Homer, the *Iliad*. The Greeks and Trojans were at war for some years. In about 1200 BC the Greeks stopped besieging the city of Troy and apparently disappeared, leaving behind them a huge wooden horse. At night, while the Trojans slept, Greek soldiers who had been hiding inside the horse, slipped out from inside it, killed the Trojan sentries and let the waiting Greek soldiers inside the city. Soon Troy was destroyed. Although the city of Troy did exist, and the war did take place, the legend of the Trojan Horse may be just that — a legend.

Why do we have hiccups?

You've probably heard of lots of cures for hiccups, some of which may work once or twice, and some of which may not work at all. For example, giving someone with hiccups a sudden shock, putting something cold down their back, or even drinking a glass of water upside down from the wrong side of the glass have all been suggested as cures. But what causes hiccups in the first place?

When you eat very hot food, it may irritate a passage inside you, or you may have a build-up of gas in your stomach, which presses against the *diaphragm*. The diaphragm is an organ which separates your chest from your stomach. It tightens up and pulls air into the lungs. But because it has tightened up, the air can't get through all the way to the lungs, and it is stopped short by the diaphragm. We feel a bump when this happens, and describe the bumping feeling as hiccuping. So hiccups are a way of telling us that the body is trying to get rid of the hot food or gas in the stomach.

Why is the word *love* used in tennis?

Long ago, no-score was indicated on French tennis scorecards by an egg-shaped zero. This was known as *"l'oeuf"*, the French word for egg, and the English-speaking players used the same word, but in this case it sounded like *love*, and has been called love ever since.

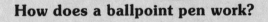

How does a ballpoint pen work?

The tip of a ballpoint pen, the part that writes, is a very tiny metal ball in a socket. As you write, the ball spins, so that the ink is put evenly on to the paper. The side of the ball which you can't see is in contact with the cylinder which holds the ink, so that ink always moves evenly over the ball and makes the pen write smoothly.

What is a mammal?

People are mammals, and so are lions, elephants, whales, pigs and rabbits. How do we know? Well, scientists have sets of rules which tell them what sort of animals creatures are: whether they are mammals, fish, reptiles, amphibians, birds or insects. There are two things which tell the scientists that an animal is a mammal. Firstly, all mammals have some hair on their bodies, and secondly, all mammals have glands called mammary glands which produce milk for their babies to drink during the early stages of life. This word 'mammary' is what gives us the word 'mammal'. The whale, the dolphin and the porpoise may look more like fish than mammals, but there is always some hair on their bodies, however small the amount, and they suckle their young with their own milk. The duck-billed platypus is perhaps the strangest mammal of them all. It has a beak instead of lips, and it lays eggs rather than giving birth, like people do, to live young. But it is a mammal. After the babies are hatched, the platypus feeds its young with milk it produces itself, and as it also has body hair, we know that it is a mammal.

What are flatfish?

Flatfish is a name given to a family of fishes which includes turbot, halibut, plaice and flounders. The flatfish have a very interesting feature which sets them apart from other fish. They have both eyes on one side of their heads. They are not born like this, but develop this feature soon after they are born. Why? Well, as the name suggests, flatfish spend most of their time lying flat on the bottom of the sea bed. To enable them to see in this position with both eyes, the eye on the lower side of the head moves up gradually to join the other on the upper side, which gives the fish a most peculiar look! As well as the eye, the fish's mouth also moves slightly, but the lopsided grin this produces doesn't stop members of this family from being very popular as food!

What is dust?

The most common sort of dust is the sort you wipe off tables and shelves, but this isn't the only sort by any means. Dust is tiny particles of solid matter, which are so light that they can be blown about by air currents. Almost everything produces dust, even the sea. This sea dust takes the form of salt dust, caused when sea spray evaporates in the air and leaves tiny particles of salt flying about. This is why when you are at the seaside, and the wind is rough, causing spray, you can taste the salt in the air. You've probably heard of dust storms, which happen in dry areas where the lack of water means that plants and grasses don't grow. The dust on the ground is blown about by the wind, and can be carried for miles, in fact, dust from the Sahara Desert has been known to fall on London. Did you know that you can actually see dust as it flies about? You see tiny particles of something moving about in a beam of sunlight – these are what is called dust 'motes', and by trying to count them you can see what a lot of dust there is in the air.

What is coal?

You may have a coal fire in your house, or you may know someone who has, and you probably don't think twice about putting lumps of black coal on to the fire to keep you warm. But did you know that coal is made of fossilised plants?

About three hundred million years ago, the land was very swampy and covered with thick forests. As the trees died, they fell into the water of the swamps, which was very acid and stopped the trees from rotting. The dead trees formed a thick layer on the bottom of the swamps, and the swamps themselves were later flooded by the sea. A thick layer of sand built up on top of the wood, and pushed it down so hard with its weight that the wood gradually hardened and became what we call coal.

These days, it is still a very hard and dirty job to mine coal, and a dangerous job too. Tunnels are dug deep underground to where the coal is buried in layers called seams. The coal is packed so tightly that powerful machines have to be used in order to get it out, and there are sometimes accidents in coal mines which happen when the tunnel roofs cave in. Luckily these don't happen very often, but you might give the miners a thought the next time you throw a lump of that coal on to your fire.

What is a marsupial?

A marsupial is a mammal which has a pouch. Its baby is born at a very early stage of development, and makes its way straight away to the pouch, where it suckles. At first the baby has no powers of suction in its mouth, and so the mother's teat squirts milk into the baby's mouth at regular intervals. Marsupials are found mainly in the continent of Australasia, which includes not only Australia itself, but also New Zealand, Tasmania and a number of small islands, and also in parts of South America. The best known marsupials are the kangaroo and the koala, which, of course, are natives of Australia.

How do snails walk?

A snail is a member of the mollusc family called a gastropod, a word which means 'stomach foot', and this describes the snail very well. The foot on which the snail moves is also the base of its whole body, and the snail moves by expanding and contracting its muscles, just as we move our muscles. Because the snail's body is so soft and sensitive, like the bodies of all molluscs, it would tear easily on sharp stones or thorns in the snail's path. So the snail secretes a special sticky slime, which covers the base of the foot and leaves a trail on your garden path, and which means that the snail can move along easily without much rubbing or friction.

Why do people have hair?

Like all other mammals, human beings have hair on their bodies. The chief job of this hair is to retain the body's heat, so that we do not die of cold. A man grows hair on his face and not so much on the top of his head, while a woman has more hair on her head and far less on her face. Men also grow hair on their chests, which women do not, and the hair on a man's arms and legs is much thicker than a woman's. Humans also have fine hair in their ears and noses, and your eyebrows and lashes are, of course, body hair. It is believed that these hairs protect the delicate organs against dust and insects, which could otherwise damage them.

Who was Mrs Pankhurst?

Emmeline Goulden was born in 1858 in Manchester, England, and later married Richard Pankhurst. With his help, and that of her two daughters, Sylvia and Christabel, she formed the Women's Franchise League in 1889, an organisation which campaigned for the right of women to vote. In 1903 she formed the National Women's Social and Political Union, with the slogan "Votes for Women". Mrs Pankhurst and her daughters, and their followers, were called the Suffragettes because they were fighting for women's suffrage, the right to vote at elections. They were often roughly treated by the police, who arrested them when they used more violent methods of drawing attention to their struggle. Many of them were imprisoned, and treated very badly. Finally, however, women over the age of thirty were given the vote in 1918, and ten years later, the year of Mrs Pankhurst's death, all women over twenty-one years old had the right to vote, putting them on an equal footing with men. It seems odd to think that women were only given the vote so recently, doesn't it?

What is a shooting star?

In fact, shooting stars are not stars at all. We call them meteors, and scientists believe that they are broken fragments of comets, which still move about in space when the comet itself does so no longer. We see them when they enter our atmosphere because they leave a trail of light behind them, caused by the friction of the air on their surfaces. Most meteors are very small, but some can weigh several tons, and the vast majority of them disintegrate when they pass through the heat of the earth's atmosphere. But some meteors, the larger ones, do land on earth, and when they do we call them meteorites. There are two main types of meteor – those made of minerals, which look like rock and are called *aerolites,* and those made chiefly of nickel and iron, which we call *metallic* meteors. Although it is very rare for a meteorite to fall on dry land, scientists think that many fall to earth every day, but that they land in the water which makes up two thirds of the earth's surface. This is why we hardly ever notice when they do hit the earth.

How many kinds of insect are there?

A good question! We know that there are about one million different species of insect, but more are being discovered every day. Except for the sea, every place on earth has an insect population, and some of these insects are very useful indeed. The honey bee and the butterflies are two of the most useful, carrying pollen from one plant to another and so ensuring that the plant life on earth continues to grow properly. Other insects are dangerous to people, like the tsetse fly, found in tropical regions, which carries the germs of the disease malaria. Not all insects have wings, though most do. Fleas, lice and worker ants don't have wings, and therefore they can't fly, although fleas and lice can jump very long distances in relation to their size.

What is the most common surname in the world?

In English-speaking countries, the most common surname is what you would expect: Smith. But the most common surname in the world is Chang, with a total of more than 80 million! And the most common first name in the world? Mohammed!

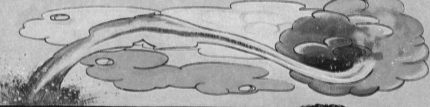

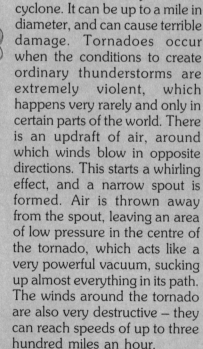

What is a tornado?

A tornado is really a small cyclone. It can be up to a mile in diameter, and can cause terrible damage. Tornadoes occur when the conditions to create ordinary thunderstorms are extremely violent, which happens very rarely and only in certain parts of the world. There is an updraft of air, around which winds blow in opposite directions. This starts a whirling effect, and a narrow spout is formed. Air is thrown away from the spout, leaving an area of low pressure in the centre of the tornado, which acts like a very powerful vacuum, sucking up almost everything in its path. The winds around the tornado are also very destructive – they can reach speeds of up to three hundred miles an hour.

What are mermaids?

Almost every sailor has a tale to tell about strange beasts he has seen in the waters of the sea, and some have told of mermaids, creatures which are half human and half fish. Fairy stories have grown out of these tales, including the most famous of all, *The Little Mermaid* by Hans Christian Andersen.

But are there really such things as mermaids? Obviously, the sailors saw something which began these stories, but was it really just as they said? Mermaids are supposed to be very beautiful sea creatures. They sit on rocks or float on the surface of the water, singing lovely and haunting songs while they comb their long hair. They have a sinister side to them as well; they are supposed to lure men down to live with them at the bottom of the sea. Of course, these poor men drown.

Nobody has ever caught a mermaid, although rewards have been offered for the first live mermaid to be caught. But the real mermaid may have been something not nearly as beautiful or as mysterious as the stories tell us.

In tropical waters there are strange creatures called manatees or dugongs, animals which look a little like very fat seals. They suckle their young on the surface of the water, and sightings of them from a distance may have been the origins of the stories about mermaids. They are not beautiful animals, but to sailors who had seen nothing but the sea, perhaps for months at a time, they appeared as something rather different from what they actually were. And the mermaids' songs? Well, have you ever heard recordings of whales 'singing' in the sea, calling to one another? It's a very strange and haunting sound, and may be the original mermaids' music. We cannot know for sure, but it seems a very likely explanation.

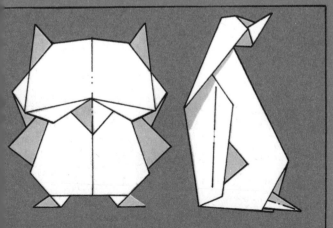

Where did origami come from?

Today we think of origami, the art of folding paper, as a Japanese craft. But the skill originally came from China, where it was the custom to make household items from paper so that they could be burnt at a person's funeral and that person could have the objects in the after life. The art reached Japan in the seventh century, and it was the Japanese who gave the skill the name origami, and perfected it.

Is there a place where the sun never sets?

In a way, this is true of the north and south polar regions, and is caused by the tilt of the earth in relation to the sun. In fact, summer at the north pole is a time when the sun never actually sets from March to September, because the earth does not tilt enough for it to disappear below the horizon. The sun does sink in the evening and rise in the morning, and during the night there is a sort of odd half-light over the polar region. Winter is very similar, in that the days as well as the nights are very dark from September to March. At the south pole, the reverse happens – summer there takes place at the same time as winter in the north, because the two poles are at opposite ends of the earth, so that when the sun is shining on one it cannot shine on the other at the same time. This is why people in Australia and New Zealand have their summer when people in Britain are in the middle of winter. It would seem strange to them to have snow at Christmas, as it would be odd for British people to eat their Christmas turkey while sunbathing on a beach!

How do we hear?

When you hit a table top with a spoon, you hear the noise it makes quite clearly. And you also feel the spoon vibrating. But you may not realise that the noise is really made of those same sorts of vibrations, called sound waves in the air, which enable us to hear the noise.

The part of the ear on the outer side of the head does very little to help us hear. But inside the ear are the delicate organs which actually do the work. The first of these is a thin skin, stretched tightly across a tube. This skin is called the *ear drum*. Behind it are three delicate little bones called the *anvil,* the *hammer* and the *stirrup.* When sound waves touch the ear drum it vibrates and makes these three tiny bones vibrate too. The bones are attached to the shell-shaped inner ear organ called the cochlea, and the bones' vibrations set up others in the fluid in the *cochlea.* Tiny cells here turn the sound waves into messages which the ear's main nerve takes to the brain, where the sounds are identified and recognised. Also in the inner ear are three other organs called the *semi-circular canals,* which control our sense of balance. If anything should go wrong with this part of the ear, we become dizzy and cannot balance properly.

What is a volcano?

You have probably read about the city of Pompeii in Italy, which was destroyed by a volcano, Mount Vesuvius, in AD 79. The reason it is important is that many things were preserved as fossils in the ash which fell on the city, and so Pompeii is a sort of museum about the Roman way of life. But what caused the volcano to erupt?

Inside the earth there is a mass of rock so hot that it is in fact liquid. In some parts of the earth, the crust – the outside layer – is cracked or thin. This means that the liquid rock inside the earth can force its way out, and form a volcano by blowing a hole in the surface of the earth. When the liquid rock bursts out of the volcano, we call it *lava,* and the volcano also pushes out ash, smoke, steam and lumps of rock with the lava. As the lava itself is still very hot and liquid when it emerges from the mouth, or crater, of the volcano, it causes a lot of damage and can destroy everything in its path by setting it on fire and then engulfing it.

Volcanoes do not occur all over the world, but there are many of them. Some are active, which means that they belch out lava and smoke quite steadily, and others are dormant or inactive. These can stay quiet for centuries, but scientists keep an eye on them in case they should suddenly erupt.

What is a unicorn?

On the royal coat of arms of Britain there are two creatures, one on either side of the shield. One animal is, of course, the lion and the other is a strange, horse-like creature with a long elegant horn on its forehead. This is the unicorn. It is a creature of legend, and probably never existed; the tales of it brought back by ancient travellers were probably the result of sightings of rhinoceroses and a good deal of imagination. Nowadays, nobody believes in the unicorn except as a legendary animal, and an heraldic beast, but years ago people did believe in its existence. Queen Elizabeth the First was supposed to have possessed a unicorn's horn, which was worth an enormous sum of money, and the horn was supposed to have healing powers and could protect people against poison. There were special rules laid down about how to catch a unicorn. A young girl was the only effective bait, and the unicorn would lay its head in her lap while the hunters crept up to do their work. The unicorn became part of the British coat of arms when Scotland and England were first united under King James the First. Before that, England's heraldic beasts were a lion and a dragon, and Scotland's were two unicorns. Legend has it that the two beasts, the lion and the unicorn, were deadly enemies, and that the only way to stop them killing one another was to place them one on either side of the shield in the coat of arms, thus ensuring that they could never get at one another.

Who were the Vikings?

You have probably seen pictures or films of Vikings – that is, actors who were pretending to be Vikings. These are huge men, wearing horned helmets and burning and pillaging churches and homes with no thought for their victims. These tales were written down by the only people who could write at that time – the monks of the monasteries which were robbed and burnt down, and so history has left us with a picture of savages almost unrivalled by anyone else. But who were the real Vikings, and what were they like?

They were Danes and Norwegians, who began to come to Britain in the year 789, when local wars in their own countries drove them out. They were not Christians. Instead they worshipped old Norse (Northern) gods like Thor, Freya and Balder, and regarded Christian churches as fair game when they saw the rich gold treasures inside and realised that here was a way of becoming rich themselves. Of course, the monks who had cared for the treasures were horrified, and wrote down their own, rather exaggerated versions of what happened, which were bound to show the Vikings as worse than they really were. The kings of England at the time did all they could to halt the rising tide of Vikings who were coming in ever greater numbers to their shores; they gave battle, and when they were beaten, the English kings had to make large gifts to the invaders, which was called tribute, and which was supposed to make sure that the invaders did not return. Of course, with the prospect of such easy money, they did return, and gradually took over almost half of England, including Yorkshire, East Anglia and a large part of the midlands. The English have had Viking kings – king Canute was a Viking, who became a very devout Christian, and was a strong king. Gradually the Vikings settled down in England and became English themselves, and we still use many words that they brought to our language. The last Viking invasion was in 1066, when the king of Norway, Harald Hardrada, attacked the north of England. The English king Harold defeated him at the battle of Stamford Bridge, and was then himself beaten and killed at the battle of Hastings, only a few weeks later, by William the Conqueror, Duke of Normandy, who was himself descended from Vikings.

Who was Robin Hood?

"He stole from the rich and gave to the poor" is a favorite saying about this notorious outlaw. According to legend, Robin is supposed to have lived in Sherwood Forest with his band of Merry Men, robbing wealthy travellers and giving their gold and jewels to the poor people of Nottinghamshire and Yorkshire. The first written account of him is in *The Vision of Piers Plowman*, a poem written by William Langland in 1377, and since then legends have grown up, showing Robin as a sort of medieval superhero, although obviously these legends were well known before the poem was written. In spite of these tales, not much is known of the real Robin Hood, and some people even believe that he may be a sort of woodland spirit, since Robin was often a name given to spirits, elves and pixies. It is doubtful whether anything will ever be known about the real outlaw Robin Hood, unless some startling evidence is found, proving him to have really been what all the stories say he was.

How do spiders spin their webs?

Everybody has seen a spider's web, and admired the skill which the spider has in web making. We know that the substance used in web making is silk, which the spider makes, and that it uses this silk not only for webs but for a whole variety of other purposes. We also know that the type of web varies very much from spider to spider, but have you ever wondered how the spider spins this silk? In the spider's belly, or abdomen, are certain glands which produce the silk as a liquid. At the tip of the abdomen are spinning organs, which have many holes in them. The liquid silk is forced through these tiny holes, making it very fine and delicate, and then on contact with the air the silk becomes solid. There are different sorts of silk for different purposes — best known is the sticky silk used in webs to trap the insects which the spider eats. Then there is the non-sticky, stronger silk for the spokes of the web, which the spider uses to walk along — had you ever wondered why the spider never gets caught in its own web? There is yet another sort of silk, which is used for spinning the cocoon in which the spider's eggs are kept safe and warm until they hatch, and other sorts for making the ropes which the spider uses for climbing down from high places. So don't dismiss the common spider as just another animal — in fact, the spider is a master at its art and ought to be treated with a lot more respect.

Where is the lost kingdom of Atlantis?

We know about the lost kingdom of Atlantis through the writings of the Greek philosopher Plato. He had heard the story from people to whom the story was already a legend, so it is by no means a new tale.

Atlantis was a very rich island with a huge city, a palace and a temple on the summit, and Plato tells us that its people became wicked and were punished by having their city destroyed in a day and a night when the whole island exploded and sank beneath the waves.

A number of people have had ideas about where Atlantis was, but one thing is sure: Plato was certainly wrong about where it was, and he may have mistaken the date of the disaster. The original Atlantis may have been off the coast of Greece, and called Kalliste. About 3500 years ago, there was a huge volcanic explosion on the island of Kalliste. The people tried to get away to Crete, an island about sixty miles away, but falling lava and rocks made escape impossible, and soon a huge tidal wave crashed down upon them. This wave travelled on to the north African coast, and its effects may have been the source of the Old Testament story about Moses parting the Red Sea.

The island of Kalliste, now called Santorini, is split into two smaller islands around a seven mile wide crater which the sea has filled up. Of course, we do not know for sure if this is the original Atlantis, but it is possible, and it would certainly match the old legends of Atlantis.

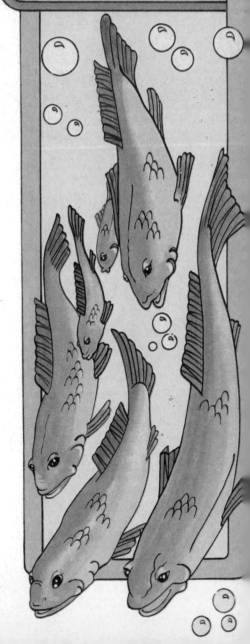

How do fish taste?

Most fish taste in what we would call a normal way – that is, they have taste buds, the organs which detect flavours, in and around their mouths. But there are some fish, in particular those that live in very dark or muddy waters, which do not feed by sight, as they cannot see their prey. These fish have not only taste buds in the mouth area, but also on other parts of their body, so that they can taste their food without actually having to swallow it first!

Are all snakes dangerous?

It depends what you mean by dangerous! Certainly, not all snakes are poisonous, and of those which are, only a very small number are dangerous to people. But in the same way that people could be said to be a danger to the things they eat, snakes are dangerous to their prey.

Most snakes kill their prey – rats, mice and other small animals – by what scientists call constriction, which means coiling round the prey and squeezing it to death. Usually the snake then swallows the prey whole; it has specially adapted jaws to enable it to swallow creatures much wider than itself.

There are only three types of snake in Britain; the slow worm is not a snake at all but a legless lizard. The first of these is the grass snake, which is not poisonous and eats mice, frogs and newts. Its size may frighten people: it has been known to reach a length of some five and three quarter feet. The second British snake, the smooth snake, is also non-poisonous. It grows only to a length of about thirty inches, and eats insects and lizards. The last snake to be found in Britain is the common viper or adder. This one *is* poisonous, but although its bite needs immediate attention, it is very unlikely that its bite would kill you. The adder usually has a long zigzag band edged with a double row of dark spots on its back, whereas the grass and smooth snakes have indistinct markings or speckles. The grass snake also has a yellowish white collar just behind its head, so you can easily tell the difference.

What causes tidal waves?

Tidal waves, or tsunami, as scientists call them, are very often the result of earthquakes on the bottom of the ocean. The sea bed shifts and slides like an earthquake on land, causing a great shock wave. Ships that are in the area of the quake feel this shock wave as if they had just struck a rock. Sometimes the shock causes a great depression in the water, and sometimes an enormous mound of water is built up very suddenly. The tidal wave builds up and travels with great speed across the ocean. Volcanoes can also cause tidal waves. In 1883 the island of Krakatoa in the Dutch East Indies was almost destroyed by a huge volcanic eruption. Great tidal waves were caused by the shock that this explosion started, and the waves made themselves felt on the coasts of Australia and California thousands of miles away.

There are warning signs on land which tell us that a tidal wave is approaching. Firstly, there is a swell like an ordinary wave. Then the sea level falls for some time, as though it were very low tide, and exposes a large area of the sea bed around the coast. Then the tidal wave, sometimes as high as two houses, comes crashing in to the shore.

What are the Northern Lights?

The Northern Lights, or Aurora Borealis, are seen in the areas near the north pole, but they are also to be seen near the south pole, where they are called the Aurora Australis. Scientists are not sure about what exactly causes the aurorae, but they think that the beautiful rays of dancing pink, green and yellow lights may be caused by sudden discharges of electrical energy from the sun, which hit the high layers of the earth's atmosphere near the poles. Here the earth's magnetic field does not protect the atmosphere from the sun's particles as it does over the rest of the planet, and so we see the lights in these regions. When they do appear, the sky may sometimes be heard to crackle, just like the noise you hear when an electric spark sometimes jumps between your hand and a glass or metal surface.

How old are rockets?

Although rockets may seem to us to be a very new invention, they are in fact very old. Not of course the type of rocket which takes people into space, but the sort we regard today as a firework. This type of rocket was known to the Chinese over a thousand years ago!

What does cold-blooded mean?

Warm-blooded creatures such as mammals have a body temperature which stays roughly the same whatever surroundings they are in. This temperature varies from creature to creature, for example the body temperature of any healthy human is 98.4 degrees Fahrenheit. Some creatures are cold-blooded, which means that the body temperature varies according to the animal's surroundings. This means that animals which are cold-blooded have to live in certain areas suitable for their survival. This is one reason why you never find cold-blooded creatures living in very cold surroundings like the polar regions – they would die of cold because they would not be able to maintain a body temperature suitable for life. Fish are cold-blooded, so are amphibians and reptiles.

How does the heart work?

The human heart is a remarkable organ. Although it is only about the size of a clenched fist, the heart is perhaps the strongest organ in the body, and is certainly one of the hardest workers. The heart is made up of four chambers, the left and right auricles and the left and right ventricles. There is a valve, like a sort of trap door, between the auricle and the ventricle on each side, which prevents the blood returning to the chamber it has just left. There are also valves between the auricles and the ventricles and the major blood vessels which are attached to the heart. Although the heart has been described as a pump, it is in fact two pumps. The left side of the heart is the first of these. It receives blood from the lungs which has a plentiful supply of oxygen in it, and it sends this blood through the arteries to the rest of the body. The right side of the heart receives blood back from the body. Now, it has far less oxygen in it and a lot of carbon dioxide waste from the cells which the body must get rid of. When this blood returns through the veins, the heart sends it to the lungs, where it gets rid of the carbon dioxide and stocks up with oxygen again as we breathe. The heart pumps the blood by squeezing itself up and relaxing. You have no control over this; the heart pumps blood around your body about 100,000 times a day, and it does so very efficiently.

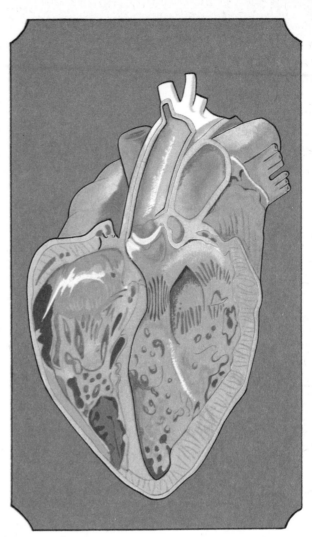

Who is Anastasia?

In 1917 the Bolshevik revolutionaries in Russia forced the Tsar, Nicholas II, to abdicate, and then imprisoned him and his family, his wife, his son and four daughters, in various places in Russia. Then in 1918 an announcement came that all the royal family, as well as four of their servants, had been killed. No bodies were ever found, and there was doubt at the time as to whether all the royal family were killed. Several people later claimed to be members of the Tsar's family, and the one who seems to have the strongest case is a woman who claims to be the Tsar's youngest daughter, Anastasia. Although some relatives of the Tsar refuted her claim, others have confirmed it. Her claim is still being urged by her friends and certain members of the Romanov family. If she is indeed Anastasia, she may be able to tell the world exactly what happened to her family, and so solve a very puzzling mystery.

The Loch Ness monster – does it exist?

The first recorded sighting of Nessie was in the year 565, when St Columba had a confrontation with the monster and ordered it not to harm people. It never has, although many people have been startled, if not frightened, by its sudden appearances.

Photographs have been taken of what people say is Nessie, and although scientists have tried to claim that the strange things shown in the photographs can be explained away as lumps of seaweed, otters diving, or old tyres, many believe that there is a creature or family of creatures living in the dark waters of the Scottish loch.

Underwater photographs have been taken which show shadowy shapes which could be the monster, and these have convinced the famous naturalist Sir Peter Scott that the creature exists. Sir Peter believes that Nessie is related to the plesiosaur, a dinosaur which was believed to have died out about seven million years ago; if this is the case, then there must be a family of monsters in the loch. One could not survive on its own. But many people will never be convinced until definite proof of the creature's existence is found, and it must be admitted that now, when monster hunting is so popular, the Loch Ness area of Scotland is almost taken over by tourists trying to catch a glimpse of Nessie. Perhaps if it *was* ever found and proof of its existence accepted, the tourist trade would slump, and although an old mystery might be solved, the people who run the Loch Ness hotels would not be too happy!

What is an albino?

An albino is a person or an animal without any color at all in their skin except the red caused by blood vessels. This is quite rare, and means that the person has very white skin, white hair and pink or red-looking eyes. The red color appears because there are lots of blood vessels in the eye. Albinos live all over the world — there are albino people in Africa, where the rest of their family is the color you would expect. As well as being striking to look at, albinos also have problems if they live in sunny countries. Because they have no color in their skin, they also have little or no protection against the harmful rays of the sun, and can burn very easily unless proper care is taken. Albinos also have no color in their eyes, which means that there is little or no protection against strong light, so many albinos have to wear dark glasses for most of the time.

How many sets of teeth do we grow?

People grow two sets of teeth during their lifetimes – the primary or baby teeth, and the second, permanent teeth.

The first primary teeth appear when a child is about six months old. The rest of them erupt between the sixth and thirtieth month, and there are only twenty teeth in this set.

The permanent teeth in humans appear between the sixth and fourteenth years of a child's life. In many cases, the children still have their baby teeth as well as the permanent set, or some of them, until they are about ten or twelve. This can look very odd, because the permanent teeth are often bigger than the baby teeth, and because the first of the second set to appear are usually the two front teeth, making the child look very peculiar. There are thirty-two teeth in the second set, although the four wisdom teeth don't usually appear until the person is in his or her late teens or early twenties. It is as well to remember that this set is the one you will have for the rest of your life, so great care must be taken to make sure that they won't go bad and have to be pulled out!

What is a cyclone?

Very simply, a cyclone is a kind of storm, and a storm is air which is moving quickly from one place to another.

A storm begins when a mass of warm, moist air from the equator meets a mass of cold, dry air from the northern hemisphere. The two masses of air will not mix — instead they form a front, which is just the name for the boundary where the two meet. The air in them continues to move, and the warm air rises above the colder air, becoming cooler as it does so. Then the moisture which was in the mass of warm air condenses and forms clouds. Meanwhile, at the center of the storm, the air pressure begins to fall, and winds blow round this area of low pressure. In the northern hemisphere, the winds blow in an anti-clockwise direction, and this means that the warm air moves north round the eastern side of the storm, and the cold air moves south around the western side.

So a cyclone is just another word for a low pressure area. Such cyclones can be enormous, sometimes about a thousand miles in diameter.

Why is hat-making called millinery?

Long ago, the best hats and headdresses in Europe were made in Milan, Italy. A citizen of Milan was called a Milaner, and although the spelling of the word has changed, a hat maker is still called a milliner, wherever he or she lives, and the hats the milliner makes are called millinery.

Why do we need water?

Very simply – because our bodies are about two thirds water. The human body contains about eleven gallons of water, and as we get rid of our body water by sweating and other means, we must replace it. The water in our bodies is not the same as ordinary drinking water, of course. There are many chemicals in it, which the body needs to grow and repair itself, and the water moves these substances around inside the body so that each part gets the amount it needs. Although on some days you may not drink as much as on others, you take in water from the solid things you eat – vegetables, fruit, meat and bread are about a third water themselves.

Blood is mainly water. About a gallon of all the water in our bodies is in the blood, but that level always remains the same, no matter how much you drink.

What is Stonehenge?

One of the stories about the time of King Arthur is the tale that Merlin the magician brought over from Ireland by magic the stones which form Stonehenge, Wiltshire, and that they were placed there to be the burial ground for Arthur's father Uther. In fact, although this a nice story, it cannot have happened. Stonehenge was already completely built fourteen hundred years before the birth of Christ, about two thousand years before the time of Merlin and Arthur. Nobody knows exactly why Stonehenge was built. It appears to us to have no use at all, but who knows what it meant to the ancient Britons? Was it a temple, a burial ground, or as has recently been suggested, a sort of early computer to calculate the movements of the stars? Unless some new information is found, no one will ever know.

Who were the first Gypsies?

In about the tenth century, groups of people began to leave northern India and to travel all over Europe. Being very independent, they kept their original language to a great extent — this is what we now call Romany, and it is a descendant of a form of Sanskrit.

Gypsies' beliefs are basically Christian, but they also have a very complicated set of superstitions and legends. Gypsies are still extremely independent, and insist on their right to live as nomads in their wagons and caravans. There are few real gypsies about these days — most of Britain's nomadic people are not fully Romany at all, but *did-dikai's*, or half-breeds, as the full Romanies call them.

What's the difference between a Star and a Planet?

A star is a huge ball of hot, glowing gases, which whirls in space. All stars are made up of the same two gases, hydrogen and helium, and they shine by their own light, which is produced as a result of atomic reactions in their center, causing great heat.

Planets are different. A planet is much smaller and more solid than a star. It does not shine by its own light, because it is not nearly hot enough to produce that light. Instead, it shines by the light of the nearest star.

Our sun is a star, and in its solar system there are nine planets — Mercury, Venus, Earth, Mars, Jupiter, Saturn, Uranus, Neptune and Pluto.

How are snakes charmed?

There is a lot of misunderstanding about this, and most of it is deliberately caused. Snake charmers would like us to believe that the snake is bewitched by the beautiful music they play on their pipes. The snake sways and dances to the music while the charmer taps his foot on the ground in time with the rhythm – and it is this tapping which solves the mystery. A snake is tone deaf; it cannot hear music, so in fact it doesn't respond to the sound of the pipe at all. But it *does* feel the tapping of the charmer's foot on the ground, and it watches the movements of the piper's swaying body so closely that it copies him and appears to dance. The music has no part in the ritual at all!